AMY-JO GIRARDIER

James

EXPERIENCE ABUNDANT LIFE

Lifeway Press®
Brentwood, Tennessee

Published by Lifeway Press® • © 2023 Amy-Jo Girardier

No part of this work may be reproduced or transmitted in any form or by any means, electronic or mechanical, including photocopying and recording, or by any information storage or retrieval system, except as may be expressly permitted in writing by the publisher. Requests for permission should be addressed in writing to Lifeway Press®, 200 Powell Place, Suite 100, Brentwood, TN 37027.

ISBN: 978-1-0877-8632-2
Item: 005842572
Dewey decimal classification: 248.83
Subject headings: RELIGION / Christian Ministry / Youth

Printed in the United States of America.

Student Ministry Publishing
Lifeway Resources
200 Powell Place, Suite 100
Brentwood, TN 37027

We believe that the Bible has God for its author; salvation for its end; and truth, without any mixture of error, for its matter and that all Scripture is totally true and trustworthy. To review Lifeway's doctrinal guideline, please visit www.lifeway.com/doctrinalguideline.

EDITORIAL TEAM,
LIFEWAY STUDENTS BIBLE STUDIES

BEN TRUEBLOOD
DIRECTOR, LIFEWAY STUDENTS

KAREN DANIEL
MANAGER, STUDENT MINISTRY PUBLISHING

AMANDA MEJIAS
CONTENT EDITOR

APRIL-LYN CAOUETTE
PRODUCTION EDITOR

SHILOH STUFFLEBEAM
& AMY LYON
GRAPHIC DESIGNERS

TABLE OF CONTENTS

ABOUT THE AUTHOR

AMY-JO GIRARDIER served as Girls' Minister for nineteen years at Brentwood Baptist Church in Brentwood, TN, and is currently serving as Women's Minister. She loves writing resources for teen girls and women and is the author of two other Bible studies available through Lifeway, *Authentic Love* and *Faithful One*.

In addition to ministry, Amy-Jo loves technology, coffee, running, serving on staff with her husband Darrel, and being with their two boys, Scout and Skylar. She is currently studying at Southwestern Theological Seminary. You can find her on Instagram: @amyjogirardier.

SPECIAL THANKS

Thank you to my husband, Darrel, and sons, Scout and Skylar, for the many sacrifices you made so that I could write. You were the ones who cheered me on and read these words first. I love you so much!

Thanks to my first girls minister—my mom, Connie Jo Morgan. Thanks to my pastor, Mike Glenn, who prays for me and cheers me on.

This study would not have been possible without the constant prayer support from what I affectionately call "TEAM AJ".

TEAM AJ: Lori Beth Horton, Catherine Horton, Bethany Horton, the Crosby Family, Bonita Wilson, Lorri Steiner, Keely and Michael Boggs, Stacey and Mark Morgan, Rachel Williams, Angela Cottrell, Chelsea Gregory, Debbie Hunter, Sarah Hathaway, Carol Vicary, Madi Weubben, Meredith Moss, Abbie Johnson, Karla Worley, Jill VanAusdall, and Rene Cook.

Special thanks to these special girls: Lexi Morgan, Kailey Morgan, Ali Scott Holmes, Joy Mina, Gracie Bechtel, Celia Tate Cook, Bella Besco, Abbey Kate Moss, Millie Moss, Wallace Memorial Student Ministry, First Baptist Church Starke Students, and all the girls and leaders at Brentwood Baptist Church who were in my heart as I wrote this resource to be used for God's glory.

And of course, thanks to the best editor in the world, Amanda Mejias. Thanks to John Paul Basham, Karen Daniel, and the Lifeway Students team for their support and hard work and for believing in me.

WELCOME

I am so glad you're here. Really! There is a team of people who have been praying for you as you start this faith adventure. This study is different from typical Bible studies. Surprise! You won't unpack every verse and passage line-by-line. Instead, we'll focus on actually living out what you are learning about. We are going to use key questions to help you understand the big themes in each chapter and how they can impact you to live your life.

The book of James is a call to action for the church. James wrote this letter to encourage the scattered, persecuted, and discouraged believers of the early church to walk in faith—faith that would be powered by the living God that was within them.

James's letter often sounds a lot like the Sermon on the Mount and the book of Proverbs. It is an invitation to apply truth to our lives, because our faith is meant to be lived out! But not through our own power—through the power of Christ in us and through us.

Over the next five sessions, we are going to have quite an adventure! I am praying that by the end of this Bible study—no matter where you are in your faith journey—you will be awakened to the adventure of living your faith in Christ and you will have surrendered to live it out by His power.

I'm praying for you as you go. He's got this, and you've got Him at work within you.

Go live it out!

Amy-Jo Girardier

HOW TO USE

For five weeks, you and your group will get together with your leader to go over the study in Group Time. You will read a whole chapter of James together—and since James is all about "painting the picture" of what it looks like to live out our faith, you'll get a chance to do some "painting" each week with a special color code just for James. So make sure you have highlighters or colored pencils ready!

- PURPLE - ROYALTY (KING)
- GREEN - GROWTH
- YELLOW - HOPE AND JOY
- RED - WOE/STOP/WARNING
- BLUE - TRIALS
- ORANGE - COMMANDS

To get the most out of this study and experience more faith adventures, I encourage you to try out the other four days that each session offers:

1. WORD STUDY

Word Study is an opportunity to learn how to dig into the chapter a little bit deeper by focusing on one word that will challenge you to live out your faith with vibrant hope.

2. IMAGE STUDY

Image Study is an opportunity to see a different "picture" that James highlights in each chapter. He is all about painting a picture for you to see what it looks like to live out your faith.

3. PRAYER EXPERIENCE

Prayer Experience is an opportunity for you to make prayer your primary strategy of living out your faith and fueling your faith adventures. In this section I'll give you some tools to put your faith in action through prayer.

4. LIVE IT OUT

Live It Out is an opportunity for you and another person (or persons) from your group to meet weekly outside of the Group Time for accountability to put your faith into action together.

Here's the fun thing: these days aren't in order! After you participate in the Group Time each week, you can choose your own adventure and pick whichever option you want to do next.

Finally, once you wrap up all five sessions, I've hidden a *BONUS GROUP TIME* in the back of the book. It's totally optional, but what better way to celebrate all you've accomplished than through a night of intentional prayer? There should definitely be some good food involved too!

Are you ready to get started? Let's go!

HEY LEADERS! DON'T MISS OUT ON THE LEADER GUIDE FOUND IN THE BACK OF THE BOOK ON PAGE 94.

SESSION 1:

Trials

Group Time

I KNOW WE'RE JUST MEETING, BUT YOU WANT TO TRY SOMETHING NEW WITH ME? LOOK AT THIS PAINTING AND LET'S PRETEND TO BE ART CRITICS TOGETHER.

This famous painting by Vincent van Gogh is called *The Church at Auvers*.[1] I first became acquainted with this painting several years ago. Of course, I was familiar with Van Gogh, but I had never seen this painting of his before. And there was something that really bothered me about what I saw.

What are some things you notice about the painting?

When I ask friends to look at this painting with me, I usually hear things like, "It's dark." "The church looks unstable." "There are two paths around the church." "There's a woman walking on the path." "The sky looks stormy." "There's no light on in the church." But do you know what I see?

Something is missing.

There's no door to the church. Why would Van Gogh paint a dark church with no door?

This question led me to do some research on Van Gogh. I discovered that, at one point in his life, he was a missionary in Belgium, where he held weekly Bible studies and ministered to the coal miners. When he saw the poverty of the miners, Van Gogh was compelled to give away everything he had to them. However, just after six months of serving, Van Gogh was fired as a missionary by the church that had sent him. Why? As Belgian pastor Luigi Davi puts it, Van Gogh was fired for "embodying the gospel in deeds, but not words." [2] Van Gogh was deeply hurt, and you can see that in his painting of a church with no door and no light.

"Yeah, that's fascinating, Amy-Jo, but what does that have to do with this Bible study on James?"

Here's the deal: Van Gogh isn't the only person painting pictures of dark and door-less churches.

> **How does this painting remind you of the way that the world paints the church today?**

An author named Brennan Manning wrote this: "The greatest single cause of atheism in the world today is Christians, who acknowledge Jesus with their lips, walk out the door, and deny Him by their lifestyle. That is what an unbelieving world simply finds unbelievable." [3]

> **Have you found this to be true inside your church? Or in the lives of Christians around you?**

As a citizen of God's kingdom, we aren't supposed to coast through life as if we have never been changed by the power of Jesus Christ. We aren't supposed to live numb towards the things of God, or just sit and wait until we go to heaven one day. Through His Word, God commands us to have a faith that is alive and active.

So what does that actually look like in our day-to-day?

As we launch into our study together, we will learn how to paint a new picture of what life in Christ looks like. James presents a string of wake-up calls to help us walk in a faith that is active, not passive. A faith that puts a light in the window and a door on the church for a hopeless world. A faith that is anchored in habits that transform everyday life into abundant life through Bible study, prayer, accountability, and real-life challenges.

So let's jump into the book of James. We're going to begin by learning about the author himself—James!

READ MATTHEW 13:55. Who is the half-brother of James?

READ JOHN 7:1-5. What did James believe about Jesus at first?

READ 1 CORINTHIANS 15:6-7 and describe what happened.

Why do you think this event is important to know as we begin our study in the book of James?

When James saw Jesus after the resurrection, it changed everything! You'll learn quickly that James will never say anything about his being the earthly half-brother of Jesus. He will, however, say everything about being the servant of God and the Lord Jesus Christ. James wrote this book to demonstrate what it looks like to follow Jesus in a culture that doesn't know Him.

Grab your highlighters or colored pencils, then read James 1:1-17. I've given you some directions on the following pages so you don't miss any of the good truths found in this passage.

¹ James, a servant of God and of the Lord Jesus Christ: To the twelve tribes dispersed abroad. Greetings.

² Consider it a great joy, my brothers and sisters, whenever you experience various trials, ³ because you know that the testing of your faith produces endurance. ⁴ And let endurance have its full effect, so that you may be mature and complete, lacking nothing.

⁵ Now if any of you lacks wisdom, he should ask God — who gives to all generously and ungrudgingly — and it will be given to him. ⁶ But let him ask in faith without doubting. For the doubter is like the surging sea, driven and tossed by the wind. ⁷ That person should not expect to receive anything from the Lord, ⁸ being double-minded and unstable in all his ways.

⁹ Let the brother of humble circumstances boast in his exaltation, ¹⁰ but let the rich boast in his humiliation because he will pass away like a flower of the field. ¹¹ For the sun rises and, together with the scorching wind, dries up the grass; its flower falls off, and its beautiful appearance perishes. In the same way, the rich person will wither away while pursuing his activities.

¹² Blessed is the one who endures trials, because when he has stood the test he will receive the crown of life that God has promised to those who love him.

¹³ No one undergoing a trial should say, "I am being tempted by God," since God is not tempted by evil, and he himself doesn't tempt anyone. ¹⁴ But each person is tempted when he is drawn away and enticed by his own evil desire. ¹⁵ Then after desire has conceived, it gives birth to sin, and when sin is fully grown, it gives birth to death.

¹⁶ Don't be deceived, my dear brothers and sisters. ¹⁷ Every good and perfect gift is from above, coming down from the Father of lights, who does not change like shifting shadows.

MAKE A PURPLE HIGHLIGHT OF 'A SERVANT OF GOD AND OF THE LORD JESUS CHRIST'

DRAW A CROWN OVER THE WORD 'LORD' (V. 1).

What does it mean for Jesus to be Lord of your life?

MAKE A YELLOW HIGHLIGHT OF 'CONSIDER IT A GREAT JOY' (V. 2)

HIGHLIGHT IN BLUE: 'WHENEVER YOU EXPERIENCE VARIOUS TRIALS' (V. 2).

Those two highlights are opposites, aren't they?

How can we have joy in trials we are experiencing?

Listen, you can't have joy in trials without Christ at work in you. But if you have faith in Christ, watch what happens.

HIGHLIGHT IN GREEN: 'KNOW THAT THE TESTING OF YOUR FAITH PRODUCES ENDURANCE' (V. 3).

Did you catch that pattern with the colors? Yellow + Blue = Green! In the same way, we can have great joy in trials knowing that Christ is at work in and through us.

Now let's string together more themes in this passage. Look back at the passage and follow the instructions below.

1. IN VERSE 2, UNDERLINE THE PHRASES 'GREAT JOY' AND 'VARIOUS TRIALS'

2. IN VERSE 3, UNDERLINE THE PHRASE 'TESTING OF YOUR FAITH'

3. IN VERSE 5, UNDERLINE THE WORD 'WISDOM.'

4. IN VERSE 9, UNDERLINE THE WORD 'CIRCUMSTANCES'

5. IN VERSE 12, <u>UNDERLINE</u> THE WORD 'TRIALS'.

6. IN VERSE 17, <u>UNDERLINE</u> THE PHRASE 'EVERY PERFECT GIFT IS FROM ABOVE'.

7. LASTLY, <u>UNDERLINE</u> THE PHRASE 'FATHER OF LIGHTS'.

8. LIGHTLY DRAW A SINGLE STRING THROUGH EACH UNDERLINING CONNECTING IT TO THE NEXT, UNTIL YOU REACH THE LAST PHRASE.

9. DRAW SOME SMALL CIRCLES ALONG THE STRING LIKE THIS ONE HERE.

There's only one thing I see when doing this activity, and it's one of my favorite things at Christmas to see—Christmas lights! (If you're feeling festive, go ahead and throw some color in those circle bulbs!)

The believers to whom James was writing were enduring hardship, persecution, separation from their homes, and countless other awful circumstances. They began questioning God's love for them instead of remembering that He was good despite how it looked or felt.

James was correcting their theology to tell them that every generous act and every perfect gift is from above. He called God the "Father of lights," a phrase which is in stark contrast to the place from which Jesus has rescued us: "the domain of darkness" (Col. 1:13). James wants Christ followers to see that God has not turned the lights out. God has not removed the door: He is at work. When things seem dark and tough, Jesus, "the light of the world" (John 8:12), shines in and through you. So trials, testing, circumstances, wisdom, circumstances—everything is connected to the "Father of lights" and they become those good gifts.

James called Christ followers to not disconnect from God, even in the things they are experiencing. He wanted them to not look for wisdom not from other places but from God. He wanted them not to blame God for their trials. He wanted them not to lose hope in their trials. He wanted them to draw near and pray. He wanted them to have their faith light up.

Friends, when you invite Jesus to be Lord and Savior of your life, like James did and like I have done, that light doesn't stay hidden. The Light of the world lights up your life, pointing others to Jesus like a string of Christmas lights lighting up a dark alley at midnight.

If you have a relationship with Jesus, reflect on your walk with Him. Can you see moments that were dark or hard yet know He was at work and shined through you? Discuss some of those moments with your group, and write them down in the Christmas light bulbs below.

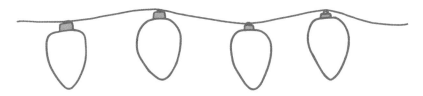

Think about your life as it is right now. How might you be tempted to feel like God has forgotten you or turned out the lights on you? Write two examples in the boxes below, and share what you wrote in one of the boxes.

Oftentimes we can forget how God was at work in our past, so we stuff our current situations and circumstances and trials in a box that we lug around in our hearts. But what if we invite Jesus to take all the things we wrote in these boxes and ask Him to carry them for us? Meanwhile, we can start praying for Him to remind us: "He is good; He is at work; He gives good gifts, and He is God."

THIS WEEK'S ICON

EACH WEEK, WE WILL HAVE AN ICON TO REMIND US WHAT WE STUDIED. TODAY IT'S A CHRISTMAS LIGHT.

Draw a single Christmas light on your hand to remind you to ask God throughout this week to shine through whatever you are enduring.

Pray in pairs for how God will use this study to shine His love to others.

WORD STUDY

Have you ever heard someone say "hashtag blessed" or heard the phrase, "Too blessed to be stressed"?

We throw around the word "blessed" a lot. But have you really stopped to think about what it means? And specifically what it means to those who are Christ followers?

READ JAMES 1:12 AND WRITE THE VERSE IN THE SPACE BELOW.

As we read the book of James, we have to understand the context of this letter. James wrote this letter much like Jewish wisdom literature was written—it reads like a list of proverbs. But these verses also reflect the format of a section of Jesus's teachings during His Sermon on the Mount.

READ MATTHEW 5:3-12.

> What similarities do you notice between this passage from the Sermon on the Mount and James 1:12?

James is painting a picture to His followers of what it looks like to live out the Sermon on the Mount. *Makarios* is the Greek word "blessed" that we find in James 1:12. It is also the Greek word we find in each of the "blessed" statements found in the Sermon on the Mount.[4] These statements are called "macarisms" or "beatitudes."

So as you are reading James, you will run into macarisms. If it says, "Blessed are..." then it is likely a macarism. Why does that matter? Well, if you read a macarism out of context, you might as well be casually saying "#blessed," because you are missing the bigger picture.

A macarism has two key parts: 1) There is someone being offered the blessing, then 2) there is the actual blessing given. "It is a brief set of two parts: a blessing is a pronounced on a person or group, and then the reason, or blessing, provided." [5]

SEE IF YOU CAN FIND THE TWO PARTS IN JAMES 1:12.

> **Blessed is the one who endures trials, because when he has stood the test he will receive the crown of life that God has promised to those who love him.**

Who is being offered a blessing?

What is the blessing given in verse 12?

It was common during the ancient Olympics for the winner of a challenge or race to receive a crown of olive leaves. But our prize is eternal life.

An important thing to note about how James uses macarisms (and Jesus in the book of Matthew, too) is that they exist only within the context of the kingdom of God. And there are usually two paths that are presented with a macarism.

LET'S LOOK AT THEM TOGETHER BELOW. GRAB YOUR HIGHLIGHTERS!

> [12] **Blessed is the one who endures trials, because when he has stood the test he will receive the crown of life that God has promised to those who love him.**
>
> [13] **No one undergoing a trial should say, "I am being tempted by God," since God is not tempted by evil, and he himself doesn't tempt anyone. [14] But each person is tempted when he is drawn away and enticed by his own evil desire. [15] Then after desire has conceived, it gives birth to sin, and when sin is fully grown, it gives birth to death.**

HIGHLIGHT VERSE 12 IN GREEN. We'll call this our "YES, let's GO!" path.

HIGHLIGHT VERSES 13–15 IN RED. We'll call this our "woe" path.

You can see the "blessing" path we painted green leads to everlasting life. This "blessing" is for those who are in the kingdom of God—which means they follow Jesus and live in light of forever with Him.

But where does that red path lead? Death. Why? Because it is where the person is pursuing a life of sin away from God. We called this the "woe" path, because not only is it not the best possible way to life, but it ends in loss, death and destruction.

So how do we make sure we are not living on that "woe" path? We need to wear kingdom glasses.

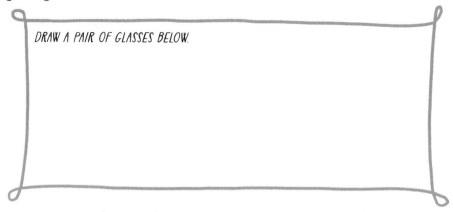

DRAW A PAIR OF GLASSES BELOW.

Do you wear glasses? If not, do you know someone who does? What's the purpose of glasses?

For some people, glasses help with nearsightedness and the need to see far away. James invites us to look at life in light of eternity with Jesus instead of what is happening right in front of us.

Glasses can also help with farsightedness and the need to see up close. James does this here by helping these believers see the good news of a life lived in the context of Jesus's kingdom.

We need to wear kingdom glasses to help us do both of these things!

PUT YOUR KINGDOM GLASSES ON FOR THE NEXT FEW MINUTES AND WORK THROUGH THE SCENARIOS I HAVE WRITTEN ON THE NEXT PAGE.

What does wearing kingdom glasses do to your frustration of not getting a lunch at the same time as your best friend?

What does wearing kingdom glasses do to the pain you are feeling right now at not getting the lead in the school play?

What does wearing kingdom glasses do to the news that you just got benched because of an injury?

What does wearing kingdom glasses do to your plans to go on spring break or go on a mission trip?

Hey, you are #blessed if you know Jesus. Just know the # should be an "H" and stand for heaven-blessed, because that is the best thing any one on earth could have or hope for each day.

Write down any areas you are stressed about right now.

How does it change your circumstances to look at them in light of living in God's kingdom?

How can you flip the script and become one who blesses others?

Draw an "H" on your hand to remind you of the kind of "blessed" you are if you are living in relationship with Jesus.

As we close out our word study today, I encourage you to ask the Lord to help you live your life with an eternal perspective and to pray for opportunities to be on mission for the kingdom of God this week. Is there someone in the midst of what you are going through who does not know Jesus? What a blessing you would be to them if you pointed them to Christ.

IMAGE STUDY

I am a visual learner—it's just how my brain works. That is one of the things I love about the book of James: he used word pictures to help provide vision for the scattered Christ followers. Jesus did this too; we have many instances where He used parables to help give vision to things like the kingdom of God.

James is trying to paint pictures for his readers so they will know how to endure these trials differently than someone who doesn't know Jesus.

GO BACK TO PAGE 12 AND LOOK FOR THE WORD PICTURE JAMES GIVES US IN VERSES 5-8.

DRAW YOUR VERY BEST VERSION OF WHAT JAMES DESCRIBES.

I'd love to see what you drew and for you to see what other girls have done! Take a picture of it and use the #AdventuresInJames. Tag @lifewaygirls and they might even share this masterpiece you've created!

Find a spot in your art to write out things you think people would say if they were stuck in that surging sea (such as, "Help me!").

What I wouldn't imagine someone yelling out for is, "God, give me wisdom to understand this, You, life, or Your mission for the church!" Yet that is what James says to do.

READ JAMES 1:5-6.

If you don't know what to do in a trial, what do you lack?

Whom does James say you should ask?

Why does doubting send us into a surging sea?

Doubting sends us into a surging sea because we aren't anchored to anything! James wants the reader to anchor onto God and draw near to Him, not to just any passing possibility or scrap-of-driftwood plan. He wants to remind his readers that Christ is with them, in them, and available to them to provide the anchor in the midst of the instability they are going through.

As we close this day today, draw an anchor on one hand and a wave on the other.

Is there a situation where you feel as if you are floating out in the ocean getting tossed around?

Close out this time by asking the Lord to anchor you. Surrender your control to Him and ask Him for wisdom.

The thing about the surging waves is that the One you are praying to is the One who calms the waves and walks on water. He's got this, and He's got you.

PRAYER EXPERIENCE

I am really excited about this faith adventure we will take each week. It is one that is extremely important, yet we oftentimes don't make time for it: prayer.

I have really grown in this adventure over the last few years. I have seen the Lord do amazing things as I have started growing in the habit of praying Scripture and praying for others. We shouldn't be surprised that when we draw close to Him, we start to look more like Him.

Around our church, we say: "Prayer is our primary strategy." Today I want to help you develop your own prayer strategy by looking at one strategy James shows us.

READ JAMES 1:5 BELOW:

Now if any of you lacks wisdom, he should ask God — who gives to all generously and ungrudgingly — and it will be given to him.

Let's be clear. This is not saying that if you start praying for that one boy you like to text you to go out on a date, God will give it to you. James is talking about wisdom!

JAMES HAD A NICKNAME THAT HAD TO DO WITH PRAYER. THERE ARE SOME ANCIENT CHURCH HISTORIANS THAT SAY HIS 'NICKNAME WAS 'CAMEL-KNEES,' BECAUSE OF THE CALLUSES HE HAD ON HIS KNEES FROM SPENDING SO MUCH TIME IN PRAYER.

James is writing to Christ followers who are enduring trials, and he knows they need some handles to hang onto in the midst of the storm. James knew we would need to hold on to Jesus to be anchored down. One way we do that is by talking with Him in prayer about His Word.

Have you ever done a Mad Lib? It lets you fill in the blanks with what you think would fit best! I used to do these all the time as a teen, and I still love them! This is a great strategy for when you don't know what to pray. I've created two fill-in-the-blank prayers that you can complete when you're not sure what words to pray.

A PRAYER FOR YOUR SPECIFIC NEEDS:

Jesus, I am going through various trials: _____
_____. I also
need wisdom for _____. When we
studied James this week, the verse _____ caught my attention. It made me
think about _____.
I ask that You guide me and anchor me as I work through _____
_____. Help me to remember that
my struggle with _____ is temporary, and
help me to live on mission to share about You. I pray I would live with my kingdom
glasses on in these parts of my life: _____ and _____
_____. Jesus, I ask these things in Your holy and precious name, Amen.

- -

A PRAYER FOR THE PEOPLE IN YOUR LIFE:

Jesus, I want to pray _____ for people whom I sit with at
lunch, and I want to pray that they come to know You, if they don't already. I want to
pray for opportunities to share my great joy in You. Give me opportunities to talk with
_____ about how You have _____
_____ in my life. I also pray for _____ as they are
going through _____. Lord, help me to bless them
by _____.

Lord, thank You for putting _____ in my life. Help me
to be a Christmas light and point _____ to You. Help me to
know when and how to bring You up when I spend time with _____.
I ask all these things in Your holy and precious name, Jesus. Amen.

LIVE IT OUT

Hey friends! I am really (really!) excited about this part of the study. Coming together in a group like we did at the beginning—and will continue to do through the rest of this study—is really important. It's great to see each other and spend time digging into God's Word with each other. But I'll tell you this: growing in our faith happens best in small groups of two to three. That is where you can keep each other accountable and challenge one another more personally.

So what will you do with the one-on-one time?

- The other group members have an invitation to ask you the hard questions, and you get to do the same.

- The other group members have an invitation to pray with and for you, and you get to pray with and for them.

- The other group members have an invitation to challenge you, and you get to do the same.

- The other group members have an invitation to hear what God is doing in your life, and you get to hear what God is doing in theirs.

This is more than just friendship and catching up about life. The purpose of this is to build your faith in Christ!

So how do we start? Let's take a moment to make this official.

_____ AND _____

(it can be more than two if you need it to be!)

ARE TAKING A FAITH PARTNER CHALLENGE TO MEET

DURING THIS STUDY OF JAMES.

WE WANT TO PRAY TOGETHER AND FOR EACH OTHER. WE WANT TO HEAR WHAT GOD IS TEACHING US IN THIS STUDY. WE WANT TO ENCOURAGE EACH OTHER IN OUR FAITH. AND WE WANT TO TRY A FAITH CHALLENGE TO BUILD OUR FAITH.

_____   _____

[Sign here and say "so be it" to each other!]

Did you know "so be it" is really what "amen" means? Yep! You just began your faith challenge with a hearty "amen." What a great way to start.

- Share what you are hoping to see happen as you study the book of James.

- Discuss the type of church you drew during the Group Time. How would you describe your faith journey?

- What is one thing so far in our study of James that seemed to jump out at you or connect with you? Why do you think it did? What are you doing with that?

- James 1:17-18 says that "every good and perfect gift is from above, coming down from the Father of lights, who does not change like shifting shadows. By his own choice, he gave us birth by the word of truth so that we would be a kind of firstfruits of his creatures."

  The new birth that James is talking about here is something that happens when someone understands his or her need for a Savior, and through the gospel—the "word of truth"—responds and asks Jesus to be Lord of his or her life. If that is something you have done, this would be a great time to share with each other about that.

- How can you pray for each other this week?

FAITH ADVENTURE CHALLENGE: BE A LIGHT

As a Christ follower, whatever you may be going through is a opportunity to shine Christ to those who are in darkness. Take a moment and determine if there is someone in your "spaces"—home, school, or work, for instance—who doesn't seem to know Jesus. Share that name with your other faith partners and commit to pray for these people.

SESSION 2:

Faith Being Real

Group Time

Welcome back! Last week we started out by looking at a painting of how someone, wounded by the church, painted a church. Remember how Van Gogh painted the church without a visible door? We considered how, in today's world, there are still people who would paint a church without a door. But as we live out Christ in our lives, we can help put doors on the church for people. They will begin to see Christ at work in and through us, and church will look alive to them.

TIME TO BE REAL!

This session is all about looking at our own lives, so let's start by taking a moment to "BeReal." Maybe you've heard about the app that sends a notification to everyone at the same time with a sound and the words, "It's time to be real." When that happens, users have a limited amount of time to click a picture that simultaneously snaps the front and back facing cameras.

What if we had a spiritual app that could take a snapshot of our heart and mind instead? Would it match what we say with our life?

Before we dig into James, let's ask the Lord to send us an alert for our hearts—it's time to be real.

Use the larger space in the blank image on the right to draw, symbolize, or journal about where you are in your heart and mind right now.

James is getting ready to have his own "BeReal" moment with the church in the passages we are going to read this week. But first, I want you to see some interesting things that are going on with the people to whom James is writing his letter.

While the exact date of this letter's writing is uncertain, it is generally believed to have been written around AD 44–62.[1] So what? Well, that makes James most likely one of the earliest books of the New Testament.

What does that mean? It means we are reading a letter to the first group of Christians who were figuring out what it looked like to live life with the risen Christ at work in them and through them. Think about that! These people might have heard the Sermon on the Mount preached by Jesus Himself. Now they were the first after Jesus's resurrection who were getting to live out the gospel.

BUT LIFE WASN'T EASY FOR THE EARLY CHURCH. HERE ARE THE SPARK NOTES ON WHAT WAS HAPPENING:

1. They were hungry. (Acts 11:28 references the famine.)
2. They were persecuted. (Acts 8:1 speaks to the scattered church.)
3. They were scattered. (Because of persecution, they left Jerusalem.)
4. They were poor.
5. They were discouraged.

These circumstances were causing the church to get distracted from their purpose of living out the gospel. In fact, James has a "BeReal" moment about the disconnect between God's Word and their lives.

READ JAMES 1:18-26 ON THE FOLLOWING PAGES.

Describe the illustration James gives in verses 22-24.

[18] By his own choice, he gave us birth by the word of truth so that we would be a kind of firstfruits of his creatures.

[19] My dear brothers and sisters, understand this: Everyone should be quick to listen, slow to speak, and slow to anger, [20] for human anger does not accomplish God's righteousness. [21] Therefore, ridding yourselves of all moral filth and the evil that is so prevalent, humbly receive the implanted word, which is able to save your souls.

[22] But be doers of the word and not hearers only, deceiving yourselves. [23] Because if anyone is a hearer of the word and not a doer, he is like someone looking at his own face in a mirror. [24] For he looks at himself, goes away, and immediately forgets what kind of person he was. [25] But the one who looks intently into the perfect law of freedom and perseveres in it, and is not a forgetful hearer but a doer who works—this person will be blessed in what he does.

[26] If anyone thinks he is religious without controlling his tongue, his religion is useless and he deceives himself. [27] Pure and undefiled religion before God the Father is this: to look after orphans and widows in their distress and to keep oneself unstained from the world.

[1] My brothers and sisters, do not show favoritism as you hold on to the faith in our glorious Lord Jesus Christ. [2] For if someone comes into your meeting wearing a gold ring and dressed in fine clothes, and a poor person dressed in filthy clothes also comes in, [3] if you look with favor on the one wearing the fine clothes and say, "Sit here in a good place," and yet you say to the poor person, "Stand over there," or "Sit here on the floor by my footstool," [4] haven't you made distinctions among yourselves and become judges with evil thoughts?

[5] Listen, my dear brothers and sisters: Didn't God choose the poor in this world to be rich in faith and heirs of the kingdom that he has promised to those who love him? [6] Yet you have dishonored the poor. Don't the rich oppress you and drag you into court? [7] Don't they blaspheme the good name that was invoked over you?

JAMES 2:8-26

8 Indeed, if you fulfill the royal law prescribed in the Scripture, Love your neighbor as yourself, you are doing well. 9 If, however, you show favoritism, you commit sin and are convicted by the law as transgressors. 10 For whoever keeps the entire law, and yet stumbles at one point, is guilty of breaking it all. 11 For he who said, Do not commit adultery, also said, Do not murder. So if you do not commit adultery, but you murder, you are a lawbreaker.

12 Speak and act as those who are to be judged by the law of freedom. 13 For judgment is without mercy to the one who has not shown mercy. Mercy triumphs over judgment.

14 What good is it, my brothers and sisters, if someone claims to have faith but does not have works? Can such faith save him?

15 If a brother or sister is without clothes and lacks daily food 16 and one of you says to them, "Go in peace, stay warm, and be well fed," but you don't give them what the body needs, what good is it? 17 In the same way faith, if it does not have works, is dead by itself.

18 But someone will say, "You have faith, and I have works." Show me your faith without works, and I will show you faith by my works. 19 You believe that God is one. Good! Even the demons believe—and they shudder.

20 Senseless person! Are you willing to learn that faith without works is useless? 21 Wasn't Abraham our father justified by works in offering Isaac his son on the altar? 22 You see that faith was active together with his works, and by works, faith was made complete, 23 and the Scripture was fulfilled that says, Abraham believed God, and it was credited to him as righteousness, and he was called God's friend. 24 You see that a person is justified by works and not by faith alone. 25 In the same way, wasn't Rahab the prostitute also justified by works in receiving the messengers and sending them out by a different route? 26 For just as the body without the spirit is dead, so also faith without works is dead.

READ JAMES 1:25. *HIGHLIGHT IN GREEN* "one who looks intently."

According to this verse, what are we supposed to look at in this way?

James uses the phrase "perfect law" with the word "freedom" to indicate this is not the Old Testament law that they worked to keep perfect.

READ WHAT JESUS SAYS TO JEWS WHO BELIEVED IN CHRIST IN JOHN 8:31-36.

HIGHLIGHT IN GREEN "perseveres" in James 1:25. The CSB translates the Greek word *parameinas* in James 1:25 as "perseveres"; the NASB translates it "abides by it."

MAKE A YELLOW HIGHLIGHT OF "and is not a forgetful hearer but a doer who works—this person will be blessed in what he does"

When we draw near to God's Word, abide in it, *and* allow the Holy Spirit to transform our lives into *living it out*, we are blessed. This doesn't mean our trials disappear. It means that amid the highs, middles, and lows, we are right where we need to be— walking with Jesus.

James wants the church to know that walking with Jesus means our faith is alive! And if our faith is alive, it should show evidence.

James uses another strong word picture in James 2:26.

What does he say about a body without the spirit?

TAKE A QUICK MOMENT AND SAY THIS TOGETHER: DOING GOOD WORKS FOR JESUS DOES NOT SAVE US.

What does he say about a faith that doesn't do good works?

How does Ephesians 2:4-5 make how we are saved clear?

A faith alive in Christ will make faith visible by its works. It will point people to the gospel and give glory to God. Anyone can say, "I'm a Christian," but it's our lives that people watch. They want to see if we live out what we say with our mouths.

READ MATTHEW 7:15-20.

How does Jesus say you will recognize someone who has faith that is alive?

James gives some scenarios that should help believers consider whether their faith is growing or dead. Read the following verses and fill out the chart below:

SCRIPTURE	EVIDENCE OF A LIVING FAITH
James 1:19	Slow to anger quick to listen slow to speak
James 1:27	take care of orphans, widows unstained by the world.
James 2:1-4	not judging by the worlds standards
James 2:12	judged by the law of liberty
James 2:14	.
James 2:15-16	

Go back to the image you drew on page 27. I didn't ask you to fill in the tiny square yet, but here's the question I have for you: If that tiny square could show a picture of your faith, would it show a faith that is alive or one that is dead?

If you know your faith is alive, use the tiny square in the image on page 27 to write one fruit of the Spirit that you would ask Jesus to grow within you. (Read Galatians 5:22-23 to review the fruit of the Spirit.)

If you're not sure, or you know your faith is dead, I'd encourage you to meet with your leader or talk with your parents right after this. Share your doubts and worries, and allow your leader or parents to walk you through what it would look like to put your faith in Jesus for maybe the first time.

THIS WEEK'S ICON

OUR ICON FOR
THIS SESSION IS A
CLUSTER OF GRAPES.

Draw a cluster of grapes on your hand to remind you that evidence of Jesus being King and Savior of your life is fruit of the Spirit in you. Ask Him to help you cling to Him and to grow the fruit of His Spirit in you.

As you close, pray in pairs for how you need the Holy Spirit's help to look more like Him.

WORD STUDY

I can still remember where I used to sit for lunch in middle school. Our cafeteria overflowed into a small gymnasium with a stage. The tables were portable and could be rolled away after lunch was over. I had a group of about nine friends who would sit at the same table. But within that group, there were three of us who sat together. Turns out, odd numbers aren't the best for friendships—it seemed that someone would always have their turn of being left out.

My mom was the first to identify it for me. I remember venting one day about my frustration of not feeling like I fit in. She finally interjected and said, "Sounds like it was your turn to get left out. Hang in there, sweetie. Tomorrow is a new day." She would often also ask me about other girls who were not in our group, and I realize now that she wanted me to see beyond the kids at my own table.

Have you ever experienced what I experienced? How would you describe your experience?

Use the space below to journal about your friend group. Talk about the people you usually hang out with, what do you normally do or don't do together, and who else you wish would be in that friend group.

READ JAMES 2:1-13.

Doesn't it sound like my school cafeteria?

The Greek word that James uses in 2:9 for "favoritism" is *prosopolempteo*.

Say it with me? "Pro-soh-po-lemp-tey-o." ←

Prosopolempteo is defined as an attitude of personal favoritism. In the original language of the New Testament, it literally means to "receive according to the face." [2] Another way to say that would be to judge people based on how they look on the outside.

Now, sure, this may happen in our schools or friend circles, but in the church? Surely that doesn't happen there. (It does happen there, doesn't it?)

As you read through James 2:1-13, you'll notice that James uses family labels of "brothers and sisters" to address the sin of favoritism. No, he's not talking to his literal family. He is pointing out that through faith in Christ, believers are all brothers and sisters. This is important to understand because James is telling these Christ followers to not live with an attitude of favoritism toward others.

To whom were the Christians showing favoritism?

Why do you think they did that?

How have you shown favoritism based on someone's outward appearance?

There were poor people and there were rich people, and poor people didn't have the same opportunities that the rich people did. Perhaps, since believers were sharing what they had with each other, there was the temptation to think a person who looked a certain way might bring his or her wealth "to the table" and receive extra benefits.

Let's look at Scripture and see what God thinks about favoritism.

VERSE	WHAT DOES THIS VERSE SAY ABOUT FAVORITISM?
Romans 2:11	
Colossians 3:25	
James 2:1	
Ephesians 6:9	
Galatians 2:6	

Jesus has no favorites. We see that clearly in John 3:16, right?

Write John 3:16 out below. <u>Underline</u> "world."

Because of God's love for us, and according to James 2:8, how should we treat people?

READ JAMES 2:12-13 AGAIN.

James is saying that when you—who were once a condemned sinner—experience the mercy of Christ, then you will know how to speak, act, and show mercy to others. You cannot judge others by anything other than what you have been judged by, that is, the law of freedom.

_____ triumphs over _____.

So what does that look like for you? For our churches? For your school cafeteria? For your friend circle? Journal in the space below where you know change needs to happen in your heart and around you.

LET'S TRY SOMETHING. I WANT YOU TO USE YOUR POINTER FINGERS AND THUMBS TO MAKE AN 'L' ON ONE HAND AND A REVERSE 'L' ON THE OTHER. TURN ONE HAND DOWN, AND PUT THEM TOGETHER TO FORM A FRAME. IF YOU HELD THAT 'FINGER FRAME' UP TO EACH FACE YOU ENCOUNTERED, THE TITLE OF EACH PICTURE WOULD BE 'GOD LOVES THIS PERSON.'

Who has been hard to see using that perspective?

How can you intentionally show that person the love of God this week?

IMAGE STUDY

Have you noticed what happens when you pass by a mirror? You look. It's hard not to look, isn't it? We are fascinated by ourselves.

Mirrors are a part of our day. We head to a mirror to check our teeth after we have a salad. We use mirrors to put on makeup and fix our hair and put in contacts. Sometimes we use mirrors to write messages or remember things.

One Easter, I decided to make a dish with lamb, and I needed to put the lamb in the slow cooker super early before going to church. I didn't think about how it would look when I wrote this message in red dry-erase marker on our bathroom mirror:

REMEMBER THE LAMB.

My husband didn't know it was a message about our lunch. He thought I was being spiritual.

James recognizes humanity's fascination with mirrors, as well, and he gives two images for us to see.

READ JAMES 1:23-24.

Describe what happens with the person who looks in the mirror.

READ JAMES 1:25.

Describe what happens with the person who looks at the law.

What if I told you that both the mirror and the Bible reflect who we are?

A mirror reflects what we look like back to us. We can see things we need to fix on the outside, like lettuce in our teeth or a hair sticking up. But God's Word shows us who we are in our hearts.

I love this quote: "The person who hears the Word but does not listen is like one who sees what God has made him or her to be, the *imago Dei*, but does not let the *imago Dei* shape his or her life." [3]

Imago Dei is Latin for "image of God," and it has its root in Genesis 1:27. "So God created man in His own image; He created him in the image of God; He created them male and female."

Every time we look at ourselves in the mirror, we are looking at the one created by God and made in the image of God. However, it's when we allow the Word of God to show us our hearts that we can have our lives *shaped* by God. Isn't that cool?

FAITH ADVENTURE CHALLENGE: SCRIPTURE MEMORY

So here's a faith adventure for you this week: Choose a verse you want to memorize and either write it on your mirror with a dry-erase marker or put it on a sticky note. Each time you look at yourself in the mirror, ask the Lord to give you a hunger for His Word and ask for His Word to shape your life.

PRAYER EXPERIENCE

Have you ever had someone share a prayer request and you responded by telling him or her, "I'll pray for you"? Well, did you actually do it?

Praying for people is a way for us to put our faith into action.

READ JAMES 2:18-26.

Let's be clear about what James is *not* saying. James is not saying we are saved by our good works. Rather, when we have Christ at work within us, we are going to be compelled to be His hands and feet.

I ALSO MADE PRINTABLE TATTOOS AND WORE MY PRAYER LIST ON MY ARMS FOR THE RACE.

As we accept that Christ is the Lord of our lives, we are going to see the needs that He sees. We are going to have our hearts break for the things that break God's heart. It will be His Spirit at work within us that will move our faith into action.

But what does this actually look like?

This past year, I had a friend who asked me to run a half marathon with her. We had run one together eleven years ago, but we decided it would be fun to do again. However, this time, we didn't train together. And let me be clear, I was hating running by myself!

I needed something to distract me while I ran, so I decided that I would start praying for people. I put out on social media that if anyone wanted me to pray for them during my training over the months leading up to the race, I would write their name down and commit to pray for them.

I had a lot of people who asked me to pray. Some of them I knew, and a few of them were friends or family of friends. I assigned them each a mile number to determine the order in which I would pray for them. I already had a long list when I received a message from a church friend whose father-in-law had suffered a fall and was in a coma.

I didn't know the man at all, but how could I say no to praying? My oldest son heard about it and said, "Mom, you have to put him on the first mile so you pray for him everyday."

So I prayed for him on mile one every day.

And every training day, I would look at my list and think, "Okay God, I'm praying for this man I don't know who is in a coma. Would You wake him up?" Then, one morning, I decided to pray differently. I said, "Lord, You made him and You know him better than he knows himself. What should I pray for him today?" I felt compelled to pray that he would open up one eye.

That seemed like a weird thing to pray. But I said, "Okay, I pray that he would open up one eye." Sometime during the week, I shared that bizarre prayer with a friend. She shared it with the daughter-in-law, and eventually, I received a text saying: "Carey said you prayed for him to open just one eye. I thought you'd want to see this picture of him with one eye open, watching a TV show." And with that, my faith grew.

Prayer is action. Praying for others is a special faith adventure. I don't know why we don't do it more often and on a regular basis, but I want us to begin today.

USE THE JOURNALING TABLE BELOW TO FILL IN SOME PRAYER REQUESTS FOR OTHERS. MY GUESS IS YOU'LL RUN OUT OF ROOM QUICKLY, SO FEEL FREE TO MOVE THESE REQUESTS INTO A JOURNAL OF YOUR OWN. MAKE SURE YOU KEEP IT SOMEPLACE YOU WON'T FORGET SO THAT YOU WILL ACTUALLY REMEMBER TO PRAY FOR EACH NAME ON YOUR LIST.

Family	Friends	Enemies	People Who Don't Know Jesus	Your Leaders

LIVE IT OUT

Before we get started today, I just want you to know that I'm really proud of you for coming back together and making this time of accountability a priority.

I meet with a group of friends every week, but at the very beginning we didn't know each other. Do you know what changed that and deepened our relationship? We committed to read the same passages of Scripture each week, as well as to pray for and with each other. My hope is that over these few weeks in prayer and God's Word, you will see God do the same for you all, too.

Well, let's jump in okay?

DID YOU KNOW THERE ARE APPS WHERE YOU CAN TRACK PRAYER REQUESTS AND PRAY FOR THEM IN REAL TIME? THEN WHEN YOU'RE DONE, IT SENDS A NOTIFICATION TO USERS THAT THEY WERE PRAYED FOR.

BEGIN BY READING BACK OVER THE PASSAGES FROM JAMES THAT WE SPENT TIME IN THIS WEEK (JAMES 1:18-2:26). IT WAS A BIGGER CHUNK OF VERSES, BUT IT'S OKAY. YOU'VE GOT THIS. ONCE YOU'RE DONE, DISCUSS THE QUESTIONS BELOW.

- During Group Time, we did some work using a BeReal image. What was helpful for you during that time?

- What is one thing in our study of James this week that stuck with you? Why do you think it did? How has it impacted the way you live?

- Read James 2:18-19. How do these verses challenge your understanding of how faith and works are connected?

- What are some ways you can show your faith through your works?

- How do you make sure your motivation is driven by your faith and not by the desire for recognition or selfish gain?

- How can you pray for each other this week?

FAITH ADVENTURE CHALLENGE: FRUIT BASKET TURNOVER

Our icon this week was "grapes." Do you remember why we chose to draw "grapes" on our hand during our Group Time? We talked about how Scripture impacts our words, our prayers, and our actions, and how we treat and see others. So the challenge is this: ask Jesus to help you see opportunities to demonstrate the fruit of the Spirit to someone. Sit in a different place or talk with a different person than you normally would. You could work together on this one if you want to.

SESSION 3:

Words/ Wisdom

Group Time

What if I pulled out an elaborate-looking box, wiped off the dust that had layered over the years, and placed the box in your hands? What if I then proceeded to tell you, in a hushed voice, that you now had in your possession one of the most powerful devices in the world? The object inside this box can start wars and end them. It can build leaders and destroy them. It can spark kindness in a dark moment, and it can choke kindness out in an instant. It can lead the way to hope, and it can point someone to evil pursuits.

And now it's yours to carry through life. Your mission is to determine the protocols or protections you want in place for this device, if any.

DRAW A PICTURE OF YOUR DEVICE BELOW. DECORATE IT AS YOU WISH!

SPLIT UP INTO GROUPS OF TWO TO FOUR TO COME UP WITH THREE PROTOCOLS OR PROTECTIONS FOR YOUR DEVICE. WRITE THEM BELOW.

1.

2.

3.

Do you know what the powerful device is inside your box? Let's find out.

READ PROVERBS 18:21 TOGETHER.

Have you ever thought about your tongue like this? Share your thoughts.

Do the protocols you made still work now knowing what the item is? Why or why not?

DON'T FORGET THAT JAMES WROTE THIS LETTER LESS LIKE A FLOWING LETTER AND MORE LIKE PROVERBS. SO IF YOU FEEL A LITTLE BIT OF "WHOA-HOW'D WE GET HERE, JAMES?!" THAT'S OKAY! REMEMBER, WE'RE LOOKING FOR THEMES.

Those precautions hit a little differently when we apply them to such a seemingly harmless part of our body, don't they? And yet, we know what power comes with the tongue.

There are times where we've heard words that brought encouragement during a tough time, and there are moments where words were spoken that caused tremendous hurt to you or someone else. Or maybe there are words that should've been spoken and you're still waiting to hear them or say them. Missing words can be just as powerful, can't they?

Let's take a moment and map out where we've been lately with our words.

When have you been hurt by someone else's words? Why did they hurt?

Have you accidentally or intentionally used your words to hurt someone else? What happened? How did you make things right?

TAKE A FEW MINUTES TO READ THROUGH JAMES 3 TOGETHER AS A GROUP.

¹ Not many should become teachers, my brothers, because you know that we will receive a stricter judgment. ² For we all stumble in many ways. If anyone does not stumble in what he says, he is mature, able also to control the whole body. ³ Now if we put bits into the mouths of horses so that they obey us, we direct their whole bodies. ⁴ And consider ships: Though very large and driven by fierce winds, they are guided by a very small rudder wherever the will of the pilot directs. ⁵ So too, though the tongue is a small part of the body, it boasts great things. Consider how a small fire sets ablaze a large forest. ⁶ And the tongue is a fire. The tongue, a world of unrighteousness, is placed among our members. It stains the whole body, sets the course of life on fire, and is itself set on fire by hell. ⁷ Every kind of animal, bird, reptile, and fish is tamed and has been tamed by humankind, ⁸ but no one can tame the tongue. It is a restless evil, full of deadly poison. ⁹ With the tongue we bless our Lord and Father, and with it we curse people who are made in God's likeness. ¹⁰ Blessing and cursing come out of the same mouth. My brothers and sisters, these things should not be this way. ¹¹ Does a spring pour out sweet and bitter water from the same opening? ¹² Can a fig tree produce olives, my brothers and sisters, or a grapevine produce figs? Neither can a saltwater spring yield fresh water.

¹³ Who among you is wise and understanding? By his good conduct he should show that his works are done in the gentleness that comes from wisdom. ¹⁴ But if you have bitter envy and selfish ambition in your heart, don't boast and deny the truth. ¹⁵ Such wisdom does not come down from above but is earthly, unspiritual, demonic. ¹⁶ For where there is envy and selfish ambition, there is disorder and every evil practice. ¹⁷ But the wisdom from above is first pure, then peace-loving, gentle, compliant, full of mercy and good fruits, unwavering, without pretense. ¹⁸ And the fruit of righteousness is sown in peace by those who cultivate peace.

James 3:17

HIGHLIGHT VERSE 1 IN RED (Remember, this is our warning color!).

Who is James warning in this verse?

Why do you think teachers would be judged more strictly?

SEE IF YOU CAN FIND THE SIX METAPHORS JAMES USES TO DESCRIBE THE TONGUE. I'LL HELP BY GIVING YOU THE VERSES TO LOOK AT.

1. James 3:3:

2. James 3:4-5a:

3. James 3:5b-6:

4. James 3:11:

5. James 3:12a:

6. James 3:12b:

LET'S TAKE A MOMENT TO PRACTICE AN EXPERIMENT WITH JAMES 3:8A. I AM CONFIDENT THIS EXPERIMENT WAS NOT PRACTICED DURING THE WRITING OF JAMES, BUT IT WOULD MAKE ME HAPPY TO LET YOU TRY IT OUT LIKE I DID.

TAKE YOUR MIDDLE FINGER AND YOUR THUMB, AND MAKE A 'C'. NOW, CAREFULLY TRY TO SNEAK UP ON YOUR TONGUE AND CLAMP IT BETWEEN YOUR MIDDLE FINGER AND YOUR THUMB. AND IF YOU GET IT, SAY TOGETHER OUT LOUD - WHILE HOLDING YOUR TONGUE - JAMES 3:8, 'BUT NO ONE AMONG MANKIND CAN TAME THE TONGUE, IT IS A RESTLESS EVIL, FULL OF DEADLY POISON.'

If you tried the experiment at the bottom of page 48, you learned that it's hard to grab and tame your tongue, isn't it? James provided vivid illustrations for us to understand how our tongues can bring about destruction, specifically in the church. (Remember who James was warning in verse 1?)

James knew that while there were trials, persecution, and poverty within the church, the biggest threat was the way believers used their words.

READ VERSES 8-10 AGAIN. *HIGHLIGHT THOSE VERSES IN RED.*

It seems like there is no hope for the tongues of these people when you read that. Like, James, come on! What do you want these people to do? Just be silent?

READ VERSES 13-18.

Did you see that? James teaches that the type of wisdom we seek for our hearts is directly connected to what comes out of our mouths.

CHARACTERISTICS OF WISDOM	
Wisdom from God:	
Wisdom from the world:	

Don't miss this, sis! The kind of wisdom you seek will determine the love of your heart. A heart that seeks the wisdom of God will show a heart characterized by the fruit of the Spirit. A heart that seeks wisdom from the world is out for self and asks, "What's in this for me?" James was showing them that they were looking out for themselves instead of looking out for each other and that it was reflected in their words.

How do we seek wisdom from God?

READ HEBREWS 4:12.

According to this verse, what does God's Word offer us?

How would you describe your personal time in God's Word recently?

What do you usually notice with your words or thoughts when you aren't spending time in God's Word?

When we spend time in God's Word, our hearts are filled with wisdom from God rather than from ourselves or the world.

THIS WEEK'S ICON

SINCE I DON'T KNOW HOW TO DRAW A RUDDER, OUR ICON FOR THIS SESSION IS A SHIP'S WHEEL.

Your tongue acts like a rudder of a ship. The words it speaks shows who's in charge of your heart. It shows who's steering your life!

Get by yourself for a moment and reflect on this for a moment. Who is steering your life? Is it your mom or dad? Is it culture? Is it a friend? Is it you? Or it Jesus—the Word Himself? Write your thoughts below.

If Jesus isn't the One steering your life, I want to encourage you to talk to a leader today about what it could look like to surrender your heart and life to Him. And if you know He is steering your heart, yet you've been trying to take the wheel lately, spend some time talking to Him about it. I've provided some talking prompts for you below:

- ASK JESUS TO HELP YOU FORGIVE WHERE YOU NEED TO FORGIVE.

- ASK HIM TO HELP CORRECT YOUR WORDS WHERE YOU NEED HIS CORRECTION.

- ASK HIM TO HELP GUARD YOUR WORDS AND NOT SAY ANYTHING AT ALL.

- ASK HIM TO HELP YOU ENCOURAGE WHEN YOU NEED TO BLESS SOMEONE.

- ASK HIM TO HELP YOU BE EVIDENCE OF WHAT IT LOOKS LIKE TO HAVE THE RISEN CHRIST IN YOUR LIFE.

- ASK HIM TO HELP STEER THE CONVERSATIONS YOU HAVE TO SHARE THE HOPE YOU HAVE IN HIM.

WORD STUDY

Have you ever locked eyes with an animal that could kill you if it was able to?

If you talk with my family about the lions at the St. Louis Zoo, they will automatically tell you the story of the lioness. I'm not sure why it happened, really, but I was standing on a balcony looking into a lion pit. My husband had gone over to look for something, and I was just waiting for him to return. That's when we saw each other. The lioness looked at me with these golden eyes, and they were mesmerizing. We both just stared at each other. She was lying down at the edge of a cave, and she looked right at me.

We stared each other down for a good minute. For some reason, I swayed to the left, then to the right—just to see if she really was looking at me. At that moment, I got my answer. She sprung out of the cave and released the loudest roar I have ever heard. I immediately backed away from the railing. My husband heard the roar and came to find me. My face told him everything he needed to know, and he asked, "What did you do?"

A lion's roar can be heard five miles away.[1] Everyone in the zoo heard that roar, and I knew that roar was meant for me. I knew that lion wanted out of her cave because of me.

READ JAMES 1:7-8 BELOW.

> **Every kind of animal, bird, reptile, and fish is tamed and has been tamed by humankind, but no one can tame the tongue. It is a restless evil, full of deadly poison.**

HIGHLIGHT 'RESTLESS' IN RED FOR CAUTION.

The Greek word translated "restless" is *akatastatos*. However, there is only place in the CSB that this word is translated "restless," and it is here in James 3:8. The same word is translated "unstable" in James 1:8. But here, after James's mention of animals, this word leaves us with a picture of a caged animal. Of course, I think of a lion or tiger. I can imagine it is pacing back and forth. It's testing the fence. It's looking for a way to get out and escape. And if it does escape, get ready for the roar! It's coming for you.

HIGHLIGHT 'DEADLY' IN RED.

The Greek word for "deadly" is *thanatephoros*. It means "death bringing." [2] The image here is of a snake whose venomous bite will kill you. Doesn't that paint a clear picture? Our tongue is like a caged animal or a venomous snake.

There is a Jewish resource called the Talmud that was used—and is still used by Jews today—as a commentary to interpret the first five books of the Hebrew Bible, also known as the Torah. In the Talmud, there are stories and sayings from Jewish life that have been passed down as well. One of those sayings is about the tongue. It goes like this: "I have surrounded you with two walls, one of bone, i.e., the teeth, and one of flesh, the lips. What shall be given to you and what more shall be done for you, to prevent you from speaking in a deceitful manner, tongue?" [3]

I can see how James would have used the word "restless" here so that a group of people who were familiar with Jewish sayings and teachings would have seen the picture he was trying to paint for them.

David knew that our words escaping from our mouth can bring damage as well.

READ PSALM 141:3.

Draw a small cage on your hand, and write "Ps. 141:3" inside it.

When you see the cage during the day, put a hand to your lips and take a moment to ask the Lord to help guard your words. Ask Him to help you use your words to build others up and not be like a restless lion, looking for ways to destroy.

IMAGE STUDY

OKAY QUICK, TELL ME HOW YOU CELEBRATE YOUR BIRTHDAY?

- **What's your birthday dessert?**

- **Candles or no candles?**

- **What's your birthday dinner?**

- **Do you have any other traditions?**

- **Do you have a memorable birthday? Why?**

Birthdays are some of my most adventurous days. One birthday adventure I remember particularly was during the sixth grade. I had just started using hair spray. (This is a detail that will come in handy in just a moment, I promise.) My mom brought out my cake—a cheesecake, like usual. My family sang "Happy Birthday," then as usual, my mom said, "Make a wish and blow out your candles." Up to that moment, it was just as it had been for every birthday before. But then, something happened!

As I blew out the candles, my brother pointed at me and started laughing. My mom slapped my face and hair. All of a sudden, all I could smell was burning hair. It was my hair! I was stunned. When I had blown out the candles, a tiny flicker of the flame combined with the potent hair spray, igniting my hair. The rest was history.

Listen, I know how quickly a spark or a match can get out of hand and change the environment. And here, James paints a picture for us of how our tongue is like a small fire.

READ JAMES 3:5-6.

HIGHLIGHT VERSE 6 IN RED. **What is the warning that James gives?**

James uses this picture to show us that our tongue, this small part of our body, is capable of doing massive things. In this picture James wants us to be aware of the great destruction that a small tongue can do with the words it passes on.

Underline "the course of life" in verse 6.

Our tongue can wreck havoc in more than just isolated events. The tongue can cause damage that can follow someone for all that person's days.

Now here's the part of the story that James alludes to in verses 13-18 about what would happen when wisdom from above intersects with the words we speak. Words point to the condition of our hearts.

READ ROMANS 10:9.

Circle the two body parts that are mentioned in that verse.

We can say anything with our mouths, but our hearts will tell us if we believe what our mouths just said. Our hearts will let us know if our mouths are lying. But when our hearts believe that Jesus is Lord, and this matches up with our mouths, we have the chance to be sparks that light up the world.

DRAW A MATCHSTICK IN THE SPACE PROVIDED AND ANSWER THESE QUESTIONS:

1. Who is Jesus in your life? Does that reflect in your words?

2. Does your heart believe the words that come out of your mouth? Why or why not?

3. How do your words need to better align with your heart?

4. Who do you hope to spark a conversations with about Jesus this week?

PRAYER EXPERIENCE

I played college soccer in college. Well, I was on a Division 2 college soccer team in college. I was a walk on. I wasn't the most skilled player, but what I lacked in skill, I made up for in determination. I wanted to improve. I worked hard and stayed late on the field, and I was frustrated that I was still one of the worst players.

One night, I went out to the soccer field by myself to just kick the ball. I started talking out loud about my frustrations, and before long I had started talking to God about each one of my teammates. I started realizing that I was in a unique position on the team: I could encourage and pray for my teammates. I realized that there were people on my team who didn't know Jesus. At that point, my perspective started to shift. I still worked hard to improve my skill, but I also began to use my time while we traveled together to get to know their stories and share mine with them.

My purpose changed when it intersected with Christ. My faith was ignited: I was inspired to pray, encourage, and pursue the girls on my team with the gospel. I started praying when I was on the sidelines. I put verses in my shoes for when I was playing. I prayed for opportunities and favor with my teammates. And you know what? God answered me.

So as you begin to put your faith into action, I wanted to give you Scripture verses to start meditating on through prayer. We'll call these "proverb prayers" because they're all based on verses from Proverbs.

Set an alarm to pray one of these every hour between 9am and 5pm.

A WORTHLESS PERSON DIGS UP EVIL, AND HIS SPEECH IS LIKE A SCORCHING FIRE. A CONTRARY PERSON SPREADS CONFLICT, AND A GOSSIP SEPARATES CLOSE FRIENDS.
PROVERBS 16:27-28

Jesus, If there is someone being talked about, help me to not add to or spread news about them.

THE ONE WHO GUARDS HIS MOUTH AND TONGUE KEEPS HIMSELF OUT OF TROUBLE.
PROVERBS 21:23

Jesus, help me to remember that words are powerful. Will You give me opportunities to use my words to encourage someone? Will You give me self-control not to speak when I want to make comments?

THE HEART OF A WISE PERSON INSTRUCTS HIS
MOUTH; IT ADDS LEARNING TO HIS SPEECH.
PROVERBS 16:23

Jesus, will You teach my heart wisdom
today to know who needs hear words of
blessing from me? Then, will You give
me confidence to say those words to
the people You put on my heart?

TO START A CONFLICT IS TO
RELEASE A FLOOD; STOP THE DISPUTE
BEFORE IT BREAKS OUT.
PROVERBS 17:14

Lord, help me not to start conflict.
Help me to be a peacemaker.
Help me to know how to navigate
conversations when the battle
lines are being drawn.

THERE IS ONE WHO SPEAKS
RASHLY, LIKE A PIERCING
SWORD, BUT THE TONGUE OF
THE WISE BRINGS HEALING.
PROVERBS 12:18

Jesus, help my words
bring healing to
someone today. Who
do I need to pray for or
encourage today? Who
needs to hear a prayer,
an encouragement, or a
truth from Your Word?

THE LORD HATES SIX THINGS; IN FACT, SEVEN ARE
DETESTABLE TO HIM: ARROGANT EYES, A LYING TONGUE,
HANDS THAT SHED INNOCENT BLOOD, A HEART THAT PLOTS
WICKED SCHEMES, FEET EAGER TO RUN TO EVIL, A LYING
WITNESS WHO GIVES FALSE TESTIMONY, AND ONE WHO
STIRS UP TROUBLE AMONG BROTHERS.
PROVERBS 6:16-19

Jesus, help me to be someone who tells the truth. Help
me not to start rumors. Help me not to "stir up trouble."

A LYING TONGUE HATES
THOSE IT CRUSHES, AND
A FLATTERING MOUTH
CAUSES RUIN.
PROVERBS 26:28

Jesus, let my
compliments be
truthful and not
just words I say to
flatter someone.

ONE WITH A TWISTED MIND WILL NOT SUCCEED,
AND ONE WITH DECEITFUL SPEECH WILL FALL INTO RUIN.
PROVERBS 17:20

Jesus, help my mind think on whatever is true, whatever
is honorable, whatever is just, whatever is pure,
whatever is lovely, and whatever is commendable.

"GUARD YOUR HEART ABOVE ALL ELSE, FOR IT IS THE SOURCE OF LIFE. DON'T LET
YOUR MOUTH SPEAK DISHONESTLY, AND DON'T LET YOUR LIPS TALK DEVIOUSLY."
PROVERBS 4:23-24

Jesus, help my heart to be protected and guarded by Your truth. Remind me of who
I am in You. Remind me of my identity in You, my value in You, and my purpose in
You. Let my relationship in You move me to look like You in action and words.

LIVE IT OUT

Hey friends: high fives! I'm super proud of you for showing up and making this commitment each week to each other and to God. This is kind of where the lab work comes in. As one of my friends recently said, "If you just holding onto the wisdom of God's Word, isn't it just knowledge? When does the transformation come in?" So today you will get to share what the Holy Spirit convicted you of, broke your heart for, or encouraged you to do. Then you get to say: *Okay, let's actually live this out!*

LET'S GO AHEAD AND RE-READ JAMES 3.

HERE ARE YOUR QUESTIONS FOR THIS WEEK:

1. What is one thing in our study of James 3 that seemed to jump out at you or connected with you? Why do you think it did? What are you doing about that?

2. What steps can we take to control our tongues and to use our words in ways that honor God?

3. Can you think of any moments where you had difficulty controlling your tongue or moments where you know the Holy Spirit was helping to control your tongue?

4. How can you pray for each other this week?

FAITH ADVENTURE CHALLENGE: PRAYER WALK

Our icon this week was a ship's wheel. Do you remember why we chose to draw ship's wheels on our hands?

This week, your challenge is to put your words into action and guide yourself to have a prayer walk at your school or your neighborhood. Prayer walking doesn't mean you have to pray out loud or close your eyes while you walk (in fact, I don't advise doing that last part). Prayer walking may seem bizarre, but it is simply praying as you walk.

If you are walking through the cafeteria, who are some people you could pray for silently in your heart? Cafeteria workers or someone who needs a friend? If you are walking through your neighborhood, pray for those who live around you.

Those are just a few ideas, but you can work together to figure out the logistics of doing a prayer walk. It is simply a tangible way to put your faith into action this week.

SESSION 4:

In the Midst of the World

Group Time

IF YOU COULD BUILD YOUR OWN KINGDOM FROM SCRATCH, WHAT WOULD IT LOOK LIKE? USE THE SPACE BELOW TO DRAW IT OUT AND GIVE A GLIMPSE OF THE MANY BENEFITS AND FEATURES IT WOULD OFFER.

TAKE A MOMENT TO DESCRIBE YOUR KINGDOM TO THE GROUP, THEN DISCUSS THE FOLLOWING QUESTIONS:

What do you love about your kingdom?

What are some of the challenges in your kingdom?

What protection do you have for your kingdom?

What would you do if someone invaded your kingdom?

The truth is, we are flawed queens, and no matter how great they seem, our kingdoms would eventually unravel. Why? Because we simply made things up as we went.

When I was growing up, my brother and I decided to make a kingdom called "Ant Island." We had a bucket with a bunch of bricks and stones in the bottom, and we filled the bucket up with water. On top of the stones, we added plants and made it look like a tropical paradise. Then we got a bunch of ants—because what was Ant Island without ants?

Let's be real—we didn't have a plan for what we were doing. We just gave the ants little food areas and watched them throughout the summer. We simply made it up as we went. But the ants seemed happy and content. That is, until one day, the boys in our neighborhood came over and get involved in the Ant Island project. One boy decided that he would put another ant colony on the island, just to see what would happen. And as you can imagine, Ant Island was no longer a paradise. There was now war between the two kingdoms, and it wasn't going to end well.

Eventually, our mom dismantled Ant Island. But I haven't forgotten the lesson I learned from the experiment that summer: I was a very bad ruler of a kingdom.

As we jump into James 4, be on the lookout for the evidence of two kingdoms. There is a battle going on, and James makes the battle lines clear in order to ask us an important question: "Whose kingdom do you serve?"

TAKE TIME TO READ THROUGH JAMES 4 TOGETHER AS A GROUP.

Based on verse 1, what was happening among the Christians to whom James was writing?

If you remember, chapter 3 ends talking about peace, so the transition to talking about conflicts and fights among the church might feel abrupt. There are different opinions from commentators on whether James was addressing the church as a whole or if he was talking about each person's individual cravings and desires. What we do know is this: James is pointing out that the conflicts happening in the church were symptoms of a deeper heart issue. The conflicts were spiritual in nature.

HIGHLIGHT VERSE 4 IN RED. **What's the warning that James is giving?**

¹ **What is the source of wars and fights among you? Don't they come from your passions that wage war within you?** ² **You desire and do not have. You murder and covet and cannot obtain. You fight and wage war. You do not have because you do not ask.** ³ **You ask and don't receive because you ask with wrong motives, so that you may spend it on your pleasures.**

⁴ **You adulterous people! Don't you know that friendship with the world is hostility toward God? So whoever wants to be the friend of the world becomes the enemy of God.** ⁵ **Or do you think it's without reason that the Scripture says: The spirit he made to dwell in us envies intensely?**

⁶ **But he gives greater grace. Therefore he says: God resists the proud but gives grace to the humble.**

⁷ **Therefore, submit to God. Resist the devil, and he will flee from you.** ⁸ **Draw near to God, and he will draw near to you. Cleanse your hands, sinners, and purify your hearts, you double-minded.** ⁹ **Be miserable and mourn and weep. Let your laughter be turned to mourning and your joy to gloom.** ¹⁰ **Humble yourselves before the Lord, and he will exalt you.**

¹¹ **Don't criticize one another, brothers and sisters. Anyone who defames or judges a fellow believer defames and judges the law. If you judge the law, you are not a doer of the law but a judge.** ¹² **There is one lawgiver and judge who is able to save and to destroy. But who are you to judge your neighbor?**

¹³ **Come now, you who say, "Today or tomorrow we will travel to such and such a city and spend a year there and do business and make a profit."** ¹⁴ **Yet you do not know what tomorrow will bring—what your life will be! For you are like vapor that appears for a little while, then vanishes.**

¹⁵ **Instead, you should say, "If the Lord wills, we will live and do this or that."** ¹⁶ **But as it is, you boast in your arrogance. All such boasting is evil.** ¹⁷ **So it is sin to know the good and yet not do it.**

In verse 4, James uses strong symbolic language to call attention to the church's unfaithfulness to God. He calls the people *adulterous*, a description for someone who has taken a vow in marriage then starts a new relationship with another person to whom that person isn't married. After this strong word of rebuke, James calls attention to the two kingdoms—one where people have friendship with the world, and another where they have friendship with God.

What should friendship with God look like?

How would you describe friendship with the world?

Why can't you have friendship with both?

HIGHLIGHT VERSE 6 IN YELLOW.

If someone says, "I love you, but . . .," you only hear what comes after "but," right? That's because "but" means the first part hinges on what is about to be said.

Fortunately, the "but" in verse 6 reveals good news!

Despite the church's actions and choices to pursue friendship with the world instead of with God, what does He offer?

Put a > (a "greater-than" sign) over "greater grace."

What does that even mean? Well, first let's look at what grace is.

READ EPHESIANS 2:8.

What can someone do to earn grace?

For all of my do-ers out there, I'm sorry! Grace is a free gift. There's nothing you can do to earn it. This gift doesn't just give us forgiveness for our sins and eternal life, but it also powerfully transforms lives and enables Christ followers to love and live like Jesus, through the help of the Holy Spirit.

So what is this grace greater than? The answer is "us"—our human sinfulness, failings, and corruption. We cannot be perfect in our own power. We will never be good enough. But by the grace of God, we can live the way that James is calling the church to live.

I'll say it again. Jesus is a good King.

HIGHLIGHT THE WORD 'RESISTS' IN RED.

That word in the Greek is *antitássomai*.[1] It means "to oppose" or "to battle against." Why would God want to go to battle against the proud? Because although our pride leads us to being our own gods and kings, there's no way we can break the cycle of sin in our own lives. We need a God who has won the ultimate victory over sin and death.

The only way to break the cycle of sin is through surrender to the King of kings. In humility, we must acknowledge the King of our lives.

Draw a white flag over verse 7 and **HIGHLIGHT VERSES 7-10 WITH PURPLE.**

What does it look like to submit to God?

Why is it necessary to humble ourselves before Him?

As I've been working on this study in James, there has been a lot of media attention regarding the word "revival." There have been many news reports about worship services that have gone on for days at various Christian campuses.

What I'm learning through James is that revival is what happens out of the humility of God's people. It starts with humbly acknowledging that He is God and we are not. True revival happens when we address this question: "Who is Lord of your life?"

Two kingdoms cannot rule one body. There has to be a decision made to surrender. Because if it's you on the throne, you won't be experiencing revival. Instead, you will only experience rebellion . . . over and over again.

Ultimately, James was addressing a throne problem for the church. They knew Jesus was King, but they thought they could share His throne. But there can't be two kings on a throne.

THIS WEEK'S ICON

DRAW A THRONE ON YOUR HAND LIKE THIS ONE.

Here's the thing, sis! I don't think most of us have a problem with Jesus saving us. We just haven't understood that it means He gets the throne—fully. He is not just Savior of our lives; He is Lord over our lies.

IN THE FOLLOWING SPACE, JOURNAL ABOUT WHO IS SEATED ON THE THRONE OF YOUR LIFE. ARE YOU TRYING TO BE YOUR OWN RULER AND LORD? OR HAVE YOU SURRENDERED FULLY TO THE KING OF KINGS AND LORD OF LORDS?

_____

_____

_____

_____

_____

_____

_____

_____

TAKE SOME TIME TO COME CLOSE TO GOD AND TALK WITH HIM ABOUT THE STATE OF THE THRONE IN YOUR HEART. CLOSE IN PRAYER USING YOUR OWN WORDS. HERE IS A PRAYER I WROTE, BUT FEEL FREE TO BORROW PARTS OF IT IF IT'S HELPFUL FOR YOU:

Jesus, Your Word says in James 4:8 that if we come close to You, You will come close to us. I want that. Draw close to me, Lord. Search my heart for anything that would be unclean and remove it. I repent for taking Your place on the throne, and I surrender my heart to You. Help me to build up Your kingdom, and forgive me for anything I've done to bring hurt within the church. Remind me how much You love me. Amen.

WORD STUDY

I have a fear of snakes. *Why are you afraid of snakes, Amy-Jo?* Thanks for asking. I'd love to tell you.

One day when I was a young girl, I rode my bike up into the backyard, and when my mom called me in for lunch, I left the bike lying down by the garden. When I went back to the bike, I picked it up and started riding it. But then I felt something like a rope banging the back of my leg. I looked down, and friends, that was no rope! It was a snake—a kind called a "blue racer"—caught in my bike spoke.

I jumped off the bike, but the snake slithered after me. True to its name, it looked like a blue streak racing through the grass. Now, my brother had once told me that the only way to make snakes stop was to turn and run at them. I was terrified, but eventually, I turned and ran at it. And it worked—the snake turned and sped away from me. (Later, I learned that blue racers are pretty harmless. Their racing isn't to attack but more to distract.)

As we read James 4 this week, I can't help but think of my confrontation with that blue racer that summer and what James says about resisting the devil.

READ JAMES 4:7 BELOW:

Therefore, submit to God. Resist the devil, and he will flee from you.

Underline the word "resist."

The Greek word for resist is *anthistemi*.[2] Look at that word really closely. Do you see anything familiar? You might know what I'm talking about if you have allergies and need to take an "antihistamine"—a type of allergy medication.

If you have allergies, your body releases a chemical called a *histamine* to fight the substance causing the allergy. When histamines are released, they also cause a range of annoying symptoms, including itching and swelling. An *anti*histamine is a medicine that's taken to block these symptoms.

I have a family member who's allergic to every kind of tree except for maybe three. I can tell when he hasn't taken his allergy medicine because first he will start sniffing. The next day, he will be sneezing. Soon after that, it will settle into a cough. He has to take his medicine to block the symptoms of his allergy attack.

Think back to what we studied together in our Group Time. Do you remember what was going on in James 4? The people in the church were fighting one another. However, the real battle had nothing to do with the people in the church. There was a spiritual battle going on.

READ EPHESIANS 6:12 IN YOUR BIBLE.

In what ways have you seen Satan attacking you recently?

Most likely, you may have even seen more challenges, struggles, and distractions happening as you have started this study in James. Satan's attacks can be summarized with these "5 Ds":

- DEVOUR: SATAN LIKES TO DEVOUR REPUTATIONS
- DIVIDE: SATAN LIKES TO CAUSE DIVISION IN FRIENDSHIPS AND IN THE CHURCH.
- DISTRACT: SATAN LIKES TO DISTRACT CHRISTIANS FROM OUR PURPOSE OF SPREADING THE GOOD NEWS AND LOVING LIKE CHRIST.
- DELAY: SATAN LIKES TO GET US TO DELAY OUR OBEDIENCE TO CHRIST.
- DESTROY: SATAN WANTS TO DESTROY OUR LIVES.

As Christ followers, we often live unaware of the battle going on around us and in us. Satan, our enemy in this battle, first shows up in the Bible in Genesis 3, when sin entered the world. Thankfully, Christ was victorious in defeating sin and death, but until His return, we still battle on.

The good news is that through the resurrected power of Christ, we have the spiritual weapons given to us, through Christ, to block the attacks of Satan. Our ability to resist him comes when we put on the armor of God.

READ EPHESIANS 6:10-20.

> According to these verses, how should we prepare for a spiritual battle?

> Which pieces of the armor of God do you forget to wear or use?

> Why is the sword of the Spirit important?

The battle is real, but you have the weapons you need.

JESUS, I COME TO YOU TODAY TO ASK FOR YOUR
STRENGTH AND PROTECTION AS I BATTLE
AGAINST _____.

I KNOW THAT I AM IN A BATTLE. I NEED YOUR HELP TO
STAND FIRM AND RESIST THE DEVIL.

I PRAY THAT YOU WOULD HELP ME PUT ON YOUR SPIRITUAL ARMOR TODAY.

JESUS, PUT YOUR WORD IN MY HEART TO GUIDE ME.

PROTECT ME WITH YOUR RIGHTEOUSNESS.

GIVE ME YOUR PEACE TO COMFORT ME.

INCREASE MY FAITH AND SHIELD ME.

GUARD ME WITH SALVATION IN YOU.

AND EQUIP ME WITH YOUR WORD.

I ASK THIS IN YOUR HOLY AND PRECIOUS NAME, JESUS. AMEN.

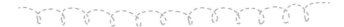

IMAGE STUDY

Yet you do not know what tomorrow will bring — what your life will be! For you are like vapor that appears for a little while, then vanishes.

When I was leading a mission journey with our student ministry in Vancouver, we had a free night and were told to take the team up by cable car to the top of Grouse Mountain to look out over the city of Vancouver. We were excited! We took the fourteen-minute ride up the mountain, stepped out . . . and saw nothing but fog.

Needless to say, we were disappointed. But you know what wasn't on the news that next day? The fog we experienced! The fog was simply there for a little while, then it was gone.

No, James wasn't a biblical-times weather forecaster. But he used fog to help the people of the church see their lives in perspective.

"You are like vapor." "You do not know what tomorrow will bring."

READ JAMES 4:13-15.

HIGHLIGHT THE WORD 'WILL' IN PURPLE EVERY TIME YOU SEE IT IN VERSES 12-15.

What was James telling his readers to do about their future?

How does this differ from the way you think about your future?

James wanted these believers to realize that their days were vanishing. So instead of wasting these vanishing days, he wanted them to intersect their lives with Christ and His will.

You get that? He's making sure that as we are living horizontally from day to day, we also add a vertical dimension to these fragile passing days we have.

So you know what that looks right, right?

> *DRAW A LINE HORIZONTALLY IN THE SPACE BELOW, THEN DRAW A LINE VERTICALLY IN THE MIDDLE OF IT.*

What would it look for you to submit your days, purposes and plans to God?

How would it change your day if, when you put your feet on the floor getting out of your bed, you considered how Christ might use you that day?

Isaiah 6:9 is my "intersection prayer" that I use to submit my day to Him. I wrote the words "Send Me" where I will see them frequently so I will remember.

Write your own prayer on a note card or sticky note, and put in a place you will see every morning or wherever you plan and schedule your days. Let this be your reminder that your days belong to the Lord!

PRAYER EXPERIENCE

Several years ago, I was invited by a missionary to lead a women's Bible study in a maximum security prison in Bangkok, Thailand. When the missionary picked me up to drive to the prison, he handed me a Bible. As I began to look at it, I said: "Sir, this Bible is not in my language."

He said, "I was told you took Spanish in college."

"I was a Spanish minor; I know a little bit."

"Well, that's more than they have now. There's a group of women who were arrested while traveling internationally and they've been asking for a Spanish translation of the Bible for Christmas. They will be so excited to hear a Christmas devotional from a Bible in their language."

As I walked into the prison, I could only take the Spanish translation of the Bible. I had to leave everything else behind. I walked to a courtyard where about twenty women were already waiting. They saw that I had the Bible.

I opened up to Matthew 1 and, in Spanish, I read verses 18-23, which tell about the nativity of the Messiah. Some of the women touched the Bible and wept.

"*Dios con nosotros*," one said.

I began to listen (the best that I could translate) to their stories of how they had come to be in prison, and how they had wanted to read God's truth in their own language.

They wanted to know more about what "*el Dios con nosostros que murió en la cruz*" —"the God with us who died on the cross"—wanted to say to their hearts. Even from a maximum security prison, these women knew that His Word could change their hearts.

James is one of the most practical books in the Bible. James knew what those women in prison knew. The God with us—Immanuel—who died on the cross and rose again changes hearts.

As we close out our time in James 4, let's use some key themes to guide us as we present our hearts to Him in prayer.

DRAW A HEART IN THE SPACE BELOW, THEN INSIDE IT, WRITE A PRAYER FROM ONE OF THESE THEMES FOUND IN JAMES 4. I PROVIDED SOME EXAMPLES BELOW IF YOU NEED IDEAS.

SUBMISSION: Jesus, You are a good King. You love me better than I love myself. And out of that love, I am safe, known, purposed, and significant. Help me to surrender and not be rebellious to Your love and lordship.

HUMILITY: Jesus, help me to acknowledge that You are King and I am not. Help me to identify when I am living pridefully.

RESIST TEMPTATION: Jesus, I have temptation before me daily. I have desires that are against the things You want for me and that would have me stray away from Your will. Guard my heart and give me Your strength to stand my ground and resist temptation.

CLEAN HANDS/HEART: Jesus, I confess my sin to You. I'm thankful that Your grace is greater than all my sin and I can bring it before You. I seek Your forgiveness. Thank You for setting me free.

WISDOM: Jesus, show me what I need to know today. Help me to have spiritual eyes to see the people You see with whom I need to talk, reach out, and be sensitive. Help me to have wisdom to say the things I need to say and not to say things I don't need to say.

LIVE IT OUT

Alright friends, how are we doing?! I hope you are looking forward to coming together and checking in on one another again. As a Christ follower who has been walking with Jesus for awhile now, I know the value and significance of having people with whom I share about our faith journeys.

GO AHEAD AND RE-READ JAMES 4 TOGETHER.

ANSWER THESE QUESTIONS TO RECAP YOUR STUDY FOR THIS WEEK:

What is one thing this week in our study of James 4 that seemed to jump out at you or connect with you? Why do you think it did? What are you doing about that?

James talks about the importance of humility and submission to God. How do you see yourself struggling in these areas at times?

James mentions resisting the devil in 4:7. What is your battle plan to help you do this? How can you help each other in this?

What are two ways you can pray for each other this week?

FAITH ADVENTURE CHALLENGE: CHOOSE YOUR OWN ADVENTURE

When I was growing up, there was a series of books called "Choose Your Own Adventure." The story would start and you would read until there was a dilemma or a challenge in the story. Then you had to make a choice about how the story should continue.

Well, this week, we're going to sort of do a "choose your own adventure" faith challenge. You get to make a choice about how you live in response to what God is doing in your life. How has He been breaking your heart for a particular mission or need? Has He shown you a certain person whom you have seen being mistreated or ignored? Maybe you can't stop thinking about sharing the gospel with someone.

Talk with your group about what God might be stirring in your hearts, then work together to help each other make a faith adventure about that. Write out your plan with two to three action steps below, then pray together through the logistics.

Now go live it out!

SESSION 5:

Patience / Prayer

Group Time

It's our last chapter in James! Give yourself a high five. Did you try it? It's really an elevated clap, isn't it? Well, hopefully you know that what we've done over these last five weeks is important and needs to be celebrated.

As we lean in today to see what James has for us in this closing passage, I want us to start with a game about beans.

1 One person gets twenty beans and each other person gets five beans. You have two minutes to exchange beans among yourselves. Go!

2 When the two minutes are up, evaluate what happened. Who has the most beans? Who has the least beans?

3 But this game doesn't mean anything right? Because beans are worthless. So let's play another round, but instead of using beans, let's use M&Ms.

4 At the end of two minutes, evaluate what happened. Who has the most M&Ms? Who has the least M&Ms? Did anyone eat some of the M&Ms?

5 Alright, last round. This time, M&M's are replaced with dollars.

6 Everyone gets one dollar, except that the one with the most M&Ms gets five dollars.

7 After two minutes of playing, answer this question: What happened when the item had more value? Who had the most dollars? Who had the least dollars?

8 The person with the most dollars gets to keep them but the challenge is: use them to show generosity!

What does it really mean to be generous?

In your own words, describe greed.

In our game, did you tend to feel generous or greedy? How did that shift
when the value of the item increased?

What makes someone tend to feel generous? What about greedy?

Ultimately, our wants and needs point to who we trust and how we trust. So what does
it look like for us to trust Jesus with our wants and needs?

Let's see what God says as we dig into our passage. James begins by addressing a
particular group of people in verse 1.

READ JAMES 5 TOGETHER WITH YOUR GROUP.

HIGHLIGHT VERSE 1 IN RED.

According to verses 2-3, what does James say will happen to their wealth in
the future?

HIGHLIGHT VERSES 4-6 IN RED.

Circle "look" and "come now you rich people" in verse 1.

It's important to know that the reason James was addressing the rich people was not
because they were rich. There are plenty of people in Scripture who had been blessed
by God with wealth. No, James is addressing the rich people because of *how* they
became rich. It's one thing for God to give you wealth, but it's completely different to gain
it dishonestly.

How did James say these people obtained their wealth?

¹ Come now, you rich people, weep and wail over the miseries that are coming on you. ² Your wealth has rotted and your clothes are moth-eaten. ³ Your gold and silver are corroded, and their corrosion will be a witness against you and will eat your flesh like fire. You have stored up treasure in the last days. ⁴ Look! The pay that you withheld from the workers who mowed your fields cries out, and the outcry of the harvesters has reached the ears of the Lord of Armies. ⁵ You have lived luxuriously on the earth and have indulged yourselves. You have fattened your hearts in a day of slaughter. ⁶ You have condemned, you have murdered the righteous, who does not resist you.

⁷ Therefore, brothers and sisters, be patient until the Lord's coming. See how the farmer waits for the precious fruit of the earth and is patient with it until it receives the early and the late rains. ⁸ You also must be patient. Strengthen your hearts, because the Lord's coming is near. ⁹ Brothers and sisters, do not complain about one another, so that you will not be judged. Look, the judge stands at the door!

¹⁰ Brothers and sisters, take the prophets who spoke in the Lord's name as an example of suffering and patience. ¹¹ See, we count as blessed those who have endured. You have heard of Job's endurance and have seen the outcome that the Lord brought about—the Lord is compassionate and merciful. ¹² Above all, my brothers and sisters, do not swear, either by heaven or by earth or with any other oath. But let your "yes" mean "yes," and your "no" mean "no," so that you won't fall under judgment.

¹³ Is anyone among you suffering? He should pray. Is anyone cheerful? He should sing praises. ¹⁴ Is anyone among you sick? He should call for the elders of the church, and they are to pray over him, anointing him with oil in the name of the Lord. ¹⁵ The prayer of faith will save the sick person, and the Lord will raise him up; if he has committed sins, he will be forgiven. ¹⁶ Therefore, confess your sins to one another and pray for one another, so that you may be healed. The prayer of a righteous person is very powerful in its effect. ¹⁷ Elijah was a human being as we are, and he prayed earnestly that it would not rain, and for three years and six months it did not rain on the land. ¹⁸ Then he prayed again, and the sky gave rain and the land produced its fruit.

¹⁹ My brothers and sisters, if any among you strays from the truth, and someone turns him back, ²⁰ let that person know that whoever turns a sinner from the error of his way will save his soul from death and cover a multitude of sins.

Let's **HIGHLIGHT IN ORANGE** the commands James gives us in verses 7-16.

1.

2.

3.

4.

5.

6.

7.

James is wrapping up a lot at the end of this letter. Why?

Go back to everything you **HIGHLIGHTED IN ORANGE**, then *UNDERLINE WITH GREEN.*

Green represents growth and life, right?

The opposite of living the way we saw in verses 1-6 is a life connected to Christ. Life without Christ is a striving for power and wealth. You will always be wanting more and more but still feeling empty. Life with Christ is resting in Him (patience), depending on him (prayer), being real with one another (honesty, confessing, and praying).

James wants the church to see that a living faith in Christ is not grasping for self but surrendering to Him.

Look at your hands. Hold one closed in a fist and leave one open.

James was talking to two groups of people in his letter: those who held onto faith in themselves (represented by your closed fist) and those who put their faith in Christ and surrendered their whole lives to Him (represented by your open hand).

This week, draw our icon using the instructions below.

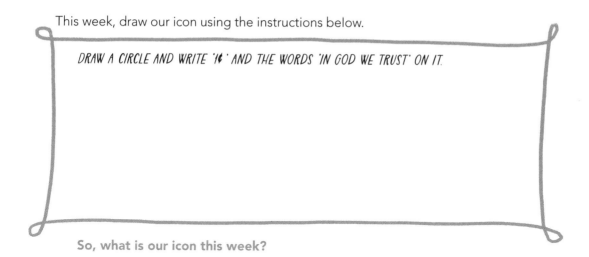

DRAW A CIRCLE AND WRITE 'I¢' AND THE WORDS 'IN GOD WE TRUST' ON IT.

So, what is our icon this week?

Isn't it interesting that of all things to have that reminder on it, it's our money? But where we put our time and money shows very quickly where we put our trust. It goes back to our bean game!

How did you play the game when the item (the beans) had no value?

What was your response when the item at play (the dollars) suddenly had real value?

If Christ has true value in your life, how will that change the way you use your time, spend your money, and live your life?

Talk with God about the people, places, and things in which you are placing value above Him. Ask for more of Him and less of everything else. Close in prayer with both hands open in surrender to Him.

WORD STUDY

When you think of endurance, what comes to mind?

READ JAMES 5:10-11 BELOW. Underline the word "endured."

> **Brothers and sisters, take the prophets who spoke in the
> Lord's name as an example of suffering and patience. See, we
> count as blessed those who have endured. You have heard
> of Job's endurance and have seen the outcome that the Lord
> brought about—the Lord is compassionate and merciful.**

That word in Greek is *hypomone*. It means to endure, to expect, or to stand firm.[1]

James is reminding us that we will need endurance just like people in the Old Testament. They had to suffer and be patient, but they were able to endure. So how did they do it? How did Job endure the suffering of sickness, losing everything he owned, his children dying, and his friends turning their backs on him?

READ COLOSSIANS 1:10-11.

According to verse 11, where does our power come from?

Why does this verse say we need power?

Here's the deal, friend: it is by Christ's power alone that we can endure. It's not a matter of "I just need to push on . . ." or "If I can try harder . . ." or "I am able to make it on my own . . ." Endurance requires a surrendered heart and full reliance upon Christ's power alone to help and to save.

James 1:3	
James 1:4	
James 1:12	

Sis, as a Christ follower, living out your faith is hard. It's heavy. The world is watching, and it needs to see how your faith in God is different. But you can't do this in your own power—and praise Jesus, you don't have to.

In the space below, journal about a situation or trial that you are having to endure right now. How are you relying on yourself to get through? What would it look like for you to rest in God's power instead? Ask Jesus to help you remember that He is at work within you to help you endure.

IMAGE STUDY

I am a city girl, but I grew up in the midwest. One of the summer jobs that we could do as a teenager was detasseling corn—removing the top from the corn plant. Why would anyone want to detassle corn? I don't know, but some people think it's a corny job. (Don't worry, that's the only corn joke I have.) This is actually a job that is still done today. The farmers need people to pull the tassels out of the corn so cross pollination will occur and the corn will produce better seeds.

The summer I had that job, I spent a lot of time talking with farmers, because we would spend the whole day in the fields, walking up and down rows, pulling tassels. Here is the interesting thing that I never paid attention to until I knew the farmers. When they planted the seeds, they wouldn't know what would happen until they harvested. They just hoped that the crop would be fruitful. One farmer told me that farming is the biggest gamble in the world. Christian farmers say it requires full trust in God to send the right amount of rain at the right times.

READ JAMES 5:7-8 BELOW. Underline "be patient."

Therefore, brothers and sisters, be patient until the Lord's coming. See how the farmer waits for the precious fruit of the earth and is patient with it until it receives the early and the late rains. You also must be patient. Strengthen your hearts, because the Lord's coming is near.

As James continues with the farming illustration, he mentions early and late rains. According to pastor and author Kent Hughes,

"The 'early' rains come in late October and early November in Palestine. Farmers still eagerly await these because they aid planting and make seed germination possible. Heavy rains come in December through February. And finally the spring rains come in April and May. These rains represent a process apart from which there can be no harvest. All farmers must patiently submit to this process. To fight against it, to bite their nails, to insist they must have fruit in the middle of the process, is futile."[2]

The farmers have zero control over when the rain comes. There is nothing they can do to make rain come sooner or later, and they don't know if there will be a harvest until it happens. All they can do is wait.

> **What's something you've had to wait for recently?**

> **Were you patient or impatient? Explain why.**

> **How do we wait well for something?**

James is asking us to wait for the return of Christ, just as the farmers wait for the rain to come. We can't control when He comes back, but we can control how we wait. So as we close out our time in today's study, I want us to turn our hearts towards thinking about the return of Christ.

> **If you knew that Jesus was coming back tomorrow, is there anyone with whom you would talk about Him? Who?**

> **If you knew that Jesus was coming back this week, is there anything you would want to do differently with your time?**

Friend, Jesus is coming back! We don't know when, but we do know He has asked us to not waste our time while we wait. Let's be intentional this week to live well.

PRAYER EXPERIENCE

To celebrate our fifteen-year anniversary, my husband and I had an amazing opportunity to go to Oahu for a few days. While we were there, we stumbled onto this extremely intriguing and challenging hike called Koko Crater Trail or, as the locals call it, "Koko Head Stairs." There are a total of 1,050 steps from the bottom to the top of the ridge.

At the very top of the trail, stuck up in the branches of a tree, there was a banged up metal tool box that was locked. The words "Prayer Box" were printed on it, and there were scraps of paper and a pen attached to the side. It was so beautiful to me! I couldn't get it out of my head the whole way down the trail. Who would put this up there? Does someone actually come up and pray for the prayers that have been put in? And most importantly, does anyone really put in prayer requests?

As we returned from our vacation, I was telling our then four-year-old son about the prayer box. We began to wonder what would happen if we had a prayer box in our neighborhood. Would anyone even use it? Would we be the weird neighbors? We had no idea, but we couldn't shake the idea that this was what we should do.

So we worked together with our friends and family to put together our prayer box. We listed the instructions and reasons for the prayer box on the side so that everyone would know that it was for our neighborhood. Then, on Memorial Day weekend, we put it out in front of our house. We prayed over it and we waited.

It took a few weeks, but all of a sudden, our neighbors began using the prayer box! Soon after that, my husband was walking around the block when someone shouted out that they had a prayer request for the box, and asked if he could pass it along.

We started realizing that we, with no intention of doing so, had put a steeple on our house just from placing the prayer box out in front of our house. It has been such a humble honor to pray for the delivery drivers, Amazon employees, neighbors, and visitors who all leave notes in our Gateway Village Prayer Box.

What opportunities might you have to put a "steeple" on your home with your family or at school? How can you be intentionally praying for others?

151 likes

amyjogirardier Got our prayer box launched today! Saw a box at the top of kokohead trail in Hawaii a year ago and felt that we could do... more

View all 7 comments

weareprayerbox ✨ 🙏🙏🙏 ✨

weareprayerbox It's incredibly encouraging to see our box inspired you to impact your own community. God bless you! He hears every word... more

MAY 28, 2016

Today, as we end our final prayer experience, I want to give you a prayer tool that someone gave me when I was in elementary school. It's called the A to Z Prayer Tool. It's for when we don't know what to pray for someone, but we want to pray prayers that line up with God's Word.

I've given you an updated A to Z Prayer Tool in the back of the book on pages 98-107 to use as a reference whenever you need it. Feel free to cut the pages out of the book and leave them somewhere you can easily access when you pray.

LET ME END BY PRAYING FOR YOU:

JESUS, I HAVE BEEN PRAYING FOR EVERY STUDENT AND LEADER WHO PICKS UP THIS STUDY— THAT THEY WOULD BE DRAWN CLOSE TO YOU AS THEY DRAW CLOSE TO YOU. I PRAY NOW THAT THEY WOULD FIND TOOLS TO PRAY FOR OTHERS AND LIVE THEIR FAITH IN ACTION IN SUCH A WAY THAT THEY POINT OTHERS TO YOU. I PRAY THAT YOU WILL HELP THEM KNOW HOW TO EXPAND YOUR KINGDOM BY TELLING OTHERS ABOUT YOU. I ASK THIS IN YOUR HOLY AND PRECIOUS NAME, JESUS.

AMEN.

LIVE IT OUT

Girls, I am not okay with this being our last time together! (I'm not crying; you're crying!)

I'm proud of you for making the commitment to Jesus and to each other. You did the thing that James talks about in chapter 5: you let your yes be your yes (see James 5:12).

As you finish this week, find a way to celebrate the journey you have taken with each other. That could be something as simple as going to Chick-Fil-A and getting ice cream together. Or it could be taking a picture together to post on Instagram and using the hashtag #AdventuresInJames, so I can see the faces of the sisters I've been praying for.

Whatever it is, do something to celebrate what you have seen God do as you have made the time to meet with Him and each other.

GO AHEAD AND READ JAMES 5 ONE MORE TIME.

HERE ARE YOUR QUESTIONS FOR THIS WEEK:

1. What is one thing this week in our study of James 5 that seemed to jump out at you or connect with you? Why do you think it did? What are you doing about that?

2. In verse 16, James talks about the importance of confessing our sins to one another. He just talked about praying for physical healing, but now he has shifted to a spiritual healing. Share areas in which you need better accountability.

3. James mentions in verse 19 that we should help each other not to stray from truth. Isn't this why we are doing this section? It's a chance to check in and make sure you are each living out God's truth in your lives. How have you seen this happen throughout your study together? Share one way you have been encouraged by knowing someone who was walking this journey of faith adventures with you.

4. How can you pray for each other this week?

This is the last week together in this study, but it doesn't have to end here!
- You can make a commitment to keep praying for each other.
- You can decide you will check back in with each other once a month.
- You can decide to renew the commitment for another five weeks.

Make sure to know what you are deciding to do, then commit to follow through. Set a clear goal and end date so that it doesn't feel impossible to achieve.

FAITH ADVENTURE CHALLENGE: SHARE THE GOOD NEWS

This is our last faith adventure and we're ending big. What is the name of the person whom you've been praying would have a relationship with Jesus? This week, I want you to make time to share with her or him about your story of how you came to know Jesus as your Lord and Savior. It doesn't have to be complicated. It can be as simple as asking her or him: "Hey, I've been thinking a lot about telling you something that is important to me. Would you have a few minutes for me to share something with you?"

You aren't alone as you share the gospel. The Holy Spirit will give you the courage and boldness as you step into that moment. Simply describe who you were before you knew Jesus. Share how you became aware that you were a sinner who needed Jesus, then explain how He is at work in your life now.

If we want to start putting doors on churches and turning the lights on, we need to tell our stories of who Jesus is to us and how we are dead without Him.

This has been an absolute blast praying and writing this study for you all. I can't wait to hear how Christ is at work in and through you all. I've been praying for you as you go. He's got this, and you've got Him at work within you.

GO LIVE IT OUT!

BONUS

Prayer Night

Friends! We made it! I'm so glad we got to do this together. By the time this gets published, I will have been praying for you for a year.

We need to celebrate in this session! Right?! What a commitment, to have gone through five chapters in James. And it wasn't easy stuff! Several times, it felt like Jesus was stepping on my spiritual toes during this study. Ouch.

Around the room we have signs with the icon for each session.

Take a moment to reflect on what you learned. Were there any sessions that you did a faith adventure or a challenge? If so, what was it and what happened?

Prayer is primary to whatever we do, which is why we want to end with a prayer experience. That leads us to our final icon: praying hands.

Here's my prayer for you, sis. As we have spent time together in James, I pray that you have seen how to put your faith in action. It is my prayer that not only have you seen how, but you have also lived out your faith through the power of Christ

I pray that you have stepped out of your comfort zone in having regular time with Jesus in prayer and Bible study. I pray that you have experienced what it's like to have a sister in Christ live out the faith with you. I pray you have seen ways the Lord has broken your heart for the things that break His heart and that you've felt called to make a difference. I pray that your school cafeterias and classrooms and homes and neighborhoods have seen evidence of Christ at work within you and that you've put "doors" and "Christmas lights" and "steeples" up on the church and in the community to point people to Jesus.

As you go, know that this is not the end. It's only the beginning of living out your faith in His power!

Leader Guide

TIPS FOR LEADING

Prepare diligently. Ask God to prepare you to lead this study. Pray individually and specifically for the girls in your group. Make this a priority in your personal walk and preparation.

Prepare adequately. Don't just wing this. Take time to preview each week so you have a good grasp of the content. Look over the Group Time and consider the girls in your group. Feel free to delete or reword the questions provided, and add questions that fit your group better.

Lead by example. Make sure you complete all of the Personal Study. Be willing to share your story, what you're learning, and your questions as you discuss together.

Be aware. If girls are hesitant to discuss their thoughts and questions in a larger group, consider arranging into smaller groups to provide a setting more conducive to conversation.

Follow up. If someone mentions a prayer request or need, make sure to follow up. It may be a situation where you can get others in the group involved in helping out.

Evaluate often. After each week and throughout the study, assess what needs to be changed to more effectively lead the study.

SCAN THIS QR CODE TO FIND ADDITIONAL LEADER ASSETS AND SHAREABLES FOR SOCIALS.

HEY LEADER!

I am so grateful to have you leading your group of girls through James! Thank you for all the prayers, time, and sacrifice that you will put into this group. Whether you have two girls in your group or fifty, God wants to work in and through you throughout your time together. As you plan this time, there are five things that will be extremely helpful to know as you prepare:

1. For each **Group Time**, you will walk girls through an overview of one chapter of James. As mentioned in the **How To** section (page 6), girls will have the chance to highlight, color, and interact with their text. You will want to bring colored pencils for the group or encourage girls to bring their own sets (they will each need their own set for the **Personal Study** days).

2. At the end of each **Group Time**, there is an icon to help the girls remember what they learned. Don't skip this section! It is sometimes referred to in the **Personal Study** days.

3. The **Session 5 Group Time** includes a game that will require supplies (beans, M&Ms, and either real or play dollars). Gather these supplies and take time to thoroughly read through the instructions of the game on page 79 beforehand—the game will be referenced throughout the Group Time discussion.

4. The **Bonus Prayer Night** on page 93 is an optional experience to add at the end of your study. If you choose to do this, it will require preparation ahead of time. You can find the instructions for the Prayer Night on page 97.

5. There are instructions for the **Personal Study** days in the **How To** section (page 6). Be familiar with these four days, because your girls could have questions. There is no order for these days, so they can have full flexibility in how they choose to complete the Personal Study. You might even need to help them plan and pair up for the **Live It Out** day.

PRAYER NIGHT INSTRUCTIONS

WHAT YOU NEED:

- 10 small containers (such as cups, jars, or baskets)
- Printed "I Am" statements (enough for each girl to get one of each). *To download the statements, scan the QR code.*
- 10 adult volunteers

SCAN FOR
'I AM'
STATEMENTS

INSTRUCTIONS:

Before your event, fill each of the ten containers with copies of one of the ten "I Am" statements. Distribute containers to your volunteers and have them stand around your room to form ten prayer stations. *(If you have fewer than ten volunteers, you may need more than one "I Am" statement per station.)*

When girls arrive, instruct them to visit each of the stations. They can go in whatever order they like so long as they visit all ten at some point during the night.

At each station, a girl will take a copy of the "I Am" statement from the container and hand it to the volunteer. The volunteer should read the verse over that girl, then hand it to her to keep. She should respond by reading the "I Am" statement out loud. If time permits, the volunteer can then pray with her. Continue until each girl has gone to all ten stations. Girls can keep the statements and refer to them on their own as often as they like.

Finish by reading James 1:2-4 and praying over the group as a whole.

A to Z Prayer Tool

ASSURANCE

Ask God for assurance of His Spirit at work in _____ so he

or she will be operating out of the Spirit's power, not out of human abilities.

PHILIPPIANS 3:3

BOLDNESS

Pray that _____ will speak the Word of God with boldness.

2 TIMOTHY 1:7

COMFORT

Ask for comfort in those times when _____ is discouraged,

broken-hearted, or stressed so he or she can pass that comfort to others.

2 CORINTHIANS 1:4

DIRECTION

Ask that _____ will be able to sense God's

specific direction in his or her ministry.

PROVERBS 3:5-6

ENCOURAGER

Ask God to send someone to encourage _____.

HEBREWS 3:12-13

FAMILY

Pray that _____ would be the kind of spouse, parent,

daughter, son, sister, brother or grandparent who pleases the

Lord and is a blessing to have in the family.

ISAIAH 40:11 EPHESIANS 5:33

GLORY TO GOD

Pray that each minute of _____'s day will be lived to glorify God.

1 CORINTHIANS 10:31

HUMILITY

Ask that _____ will develop a sense of humility rejecting pride.

JAMES 5:10 I PETER 5:6-7

INSIGHT

Ask that _____ will see people and things from God's perspective.

EPHESIANS 1:7-8

JOY

Pray that _____ will be full of the joy of the Lord in all situations.

NEHEMIAH 8:10

KNOWLEDGE

Pray that _____ will crave knowledge of God's Word and apply it consistently.

PSALM 119:105

LOVE

Ask that _____ will be a vessel through which God's love flows to others.

1 JOHN 3:16

MOTIVATION

Pray that _____ will do his or her work from

godly motives, not to please other people.

I THESSALONIANS 2:4

NEEDS

Pray that _____ will realize that in Christ, all of his or her needs will be met.

2 PETER 1:3

OPEN DOOR

Pray that _____ will recognize opportunities to

share the gospel.

ACTS 28: 30 31

PRAYER PARTNERS

Ask God to provide prayer partners for _____ — people who will

intercede on a regular basis.

2 THESSALONIANS 1:11

QUIET TIME

Pray that nothing will get in the way of _____ having

a quality quiet time with the Lord each day, in which knowing who

God is and what He does becomes a priority.

PSALM 46:10

REVIVAL

Ask God to work in _____'s life so he or she will be

willing to meet the conditions for personal revival.

2 CHRONICLES 7:14

SERVANTHOOD

Pray that _____ will do his or her work with a servant spirit.

PHILIPPIANS 2:5-7

THANKFUL HEART

Ask that _____ will learn to thank God for what

he or she is doing, even in difficult situations.

EPHESIANS 5:20

UNSAVED

Pray that unsaved people whom _____ encounters will

develop a hunger and thirst for Jesus Christ in their lives.

2 CORINTHIANS 4:45

VICTORY

Pray that _____ will know victory in spiritual warfare.

2 CORINTHIANS 10:3-5

WEARINESS

Pray that _____ will not get bogged down in having to much to do.

GALATIANS 6:9

X-RAY VISION

Ask that _____ will have X-ray vision of the heart to see

anything in his or her life that needs confessing; pray that

_____ will desire a cleansed life.

PSALM 51

YIELDING

Pray that _____ will be completely yielded

to Christ, being willing to be dead to self.

GALATIANS 2:20

ZEAL

Pray that _____ will have a renewed zeal to share the gospel.

COLOSSIANS 1:3-6

NOTES

SOURCES

SESSION 1

1. Vincent van Gogh, *The Church at Auvers*, oil on canvas, June 1890, Musée d'Orsay, courtesy of the National Gallery of Art, Washington DC, https://commons.wikimedia.org/wiki/File:Vincent_van_Gogh_-_The_Church_in_Auvers-sur-Oise,_View_from_the_Chevet_-_Google_Art_Project.jpg.

2. Luigi Davi, quoted by Mary Winston Nicklin, "In Belgium's Borinage, where Van Gogh the pastor became a painter, *The Washington Post*, February 19, 2015, https://www.washingtonpost.com/lifestyle/travel/in-belgiums-borinage-on-the-trail-of-vincent-van-gogh-the-priest/2015/02/19/b46c2c12-a731-11e4-a7c2-03d37af98440_story.html

3. Brennan Manning, as sampled by DC Talk, "What if I Stumble?", track 4 on *Jesus Freak*, ForeFront Records, 1995, remastered 2013, https://open.spotify.com/track/6amSl4oPLY4f64BoXJUyNu?si=a3cd850b88df4fb0.

4. F. Hauck, "Makários" in *Theological Dictionary of the New Testament, Abridged in One Volume (TDNT)*, Gerhard Kittel and Gerhard Friedrich, eds., Geoffrey William Bromiley, trans. (Grand Rapids, MI: W.B. Eerdmans, 1985), 548.

5. Scott McKnight, *The Letter of James*, The New International Commentary on the New Testament (Grand Rapids: Eerdmans, 2011), 107-108.

SESSION 2

1. Simon J. Kistemaker, *Exposition of James and the Epistles of John* (Grand Rapids, MI: Baker 1986), 18-19,27.

2. Douglas J. Moo, *James: An Introduction and Commentary*, Tyndale New Testament Commentaries, Vol 16 (Westmont, IL: IVP Academic, 2015), 139.

3. McKnight, *Letter of James*, 151.

SESSION 3

1. Marsea Nelson, "Ten Interesting Facts about Lions," World Wildlife Fund, June 29, 2011, https://www.worldwildlife.org/blogs/good-nature-travel/posts/ten-interesting-facts-about-lions.

2. A. T. Robertson, *Word Pictures in the New Testament*, Concise Edition, Logos version (Holman Bible Publishers, 2010), Jas 3:8.

3. Koren Noe Talmud, William Davidson digital edition, b. Arakhin 15b:5, https://www.sefaria.org/Arakhin.15b.5?lang=bi.

SESSION 4

1. J. R. Blue, "antitassomai," in *The Bible Knowledge Commentary: An Exposition of the Scriptures*, Vol. 2, J. F. Walvoord & R. B. Zuck, eds. (Victor Books: 1985), 830.

2. J. W. Hayford, "anthistemi" in *Hayford's Bible Handbook,* Logos version (Nashville: Thomas Nelson, 1995).

SESSION 5

1. F. Hauck, "ménō," *TDNT*, 582-84.

2. Kent R. Hughes, *James: Faith that Works* (Wheaton, IL: Crossway, 2015), 274, accessed on Scribd, https://www.scribd.com/read/279994282/James-ESV-Edition-Faith-That-Works.

Get the most from your study.

Customize your Bible study time with a guided experience and additional resources.

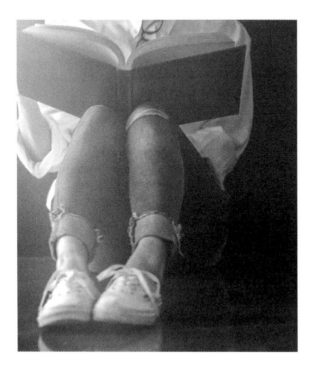

Following after Jesus shouldn't be boring. Throughout this five-session study on the book of James, you'll discover practical and transformative habits that lead to real life faith adventures. Through fun and interactive study days, Amy-Jo Girardier teaches how we can experience the abundant life by doing real life with Jesus.

For more information about Lifeway Girls, visit lifeway.com/girls.

lifeway.com / jamesteengirl